"Clean. Elegant. Delicious. Melina Davies delivers an exceptional experience with her Olive & Thyme restaurants, and now, in sharing her personal stories and techniques in her cookbook, she gives us the gift of great dishes to prepare at home for friends and family."
— KEANU REEVES, actor, publisher, and author

"With *Olive & Thyme*, Melina Davies will inspire the 'accidental' chef in everyone! As soon as you open Melina's book, you are invited into learning not just about delicious recipes that create splendid little meals with little fuss, but understanding that a love for cooking can summon our closest friends and family to spend time together around a table."
— MATT MOLINA, James Beard Award–winning chef, restaurateur, and co-author of *The Mozza Cookbook*

"I've been going to Olive & Thyme for the last eight years for breakfast, lunch, and dinner. Now, I get to have Melina's delicious food in the comfort of my own home. She's not only helping people cook tasty meals, she's solving the Los Angeles traffic problem."
— ERIC STONESTREET, actor and star of *Modern Family*

"Melina Davies' gift—*Olive & Thyme*—shares a simple, heartfelt, delicious plate of life and connection."
— DELLA GOSSETT, executive pastry chef at Spago

olive & thyme

olive & thyme

Everyday Meals
Made Extraordinary

Melina Davies

Photography by Ann Elliott Cutting
with Ashley Barrett

PROSPECT
·PARK·
BOOKS

This book is dedicated to the loves of my life:
My husband, Christian, and my beautiful children, Jagger and River.
Without your patience and love I would have never been able to follow my passion.

Mom and Dad, you taught me the meaning of hard work and sacrifice.
The traditions you imbedded in me will be passed down for generations.

I will forever be humbled to cook a meal and sit around a table with you.

Contents

Melina (center), not long before she started cooking dinner for her family.

Soulful Takes on Everyday Classics

Nancy Silverton

After a long day, a working spouse returns home and wafting aromas hit them as soon as they open the front door. The children of this family come home soon afterward, and those lingering, tantalizing fragrances greet them, too. This is a scene played out nightly across America, indeed across the world, as it did on television screens showing the folksy shows of my youth.

The gigantic difference between *Father Knows Best* or *The Dick Van Dyke Show* and the scene above was that at the home of Melina Davies in Los Angeles, the one cooking that dinner was her, and she was eight years old.

While her schoolmates were watching *Scooby-Doo*, Melina was soaking in the cooking shows of Julia Child and Jacques Pépin. She took to Julia and Jacques with an enthusiasm that would carry her through life. At that tender age, dinner became more than food; it became a family gathering where everyone talked about their day. Melina loved that. She got hooked on fine food and hospitality, and that comes through in her terrific new cookbook, *Olive & Thyme*, named after not only her own restaurant, but for two ingredients whose vitality sums up Melina and her food.

I think the beauty of *Olive & Thyme* is stated so simply in its subtitle: "Everyday Meals Made Extraordinary." This is a book you will actually cook from. It's not like the Noma cookbook. Or even some of mine, which are—hopefully—fun to thumb through but daunting to cook from.

Olive & Thyme has familiar dishes, but ones that are given, with often just a simple extra addition, a jolt that enlivens them. Check out the lemon turkey sandwich, a recipe that defines this cookbook. The key to it is simply the addition of preserved lemons. It takes a routine dish and elevates it to a different level.

And that is what I like so much about the book: familiarity, jazzed up. But not with an entire horn section or an orchestra of strings. Sometimes all it takes is a few silky notes from a sax or the soulful tinkle of the ivories. Or some chopped thyme and a few good olives.

Here's to Melina Davies and her soulful take on dishes your family will cherish.

Nancy Silverton is the chef and owner of the Mozza restaurants and Chi Spacca, as well as the author of Chi Spacca, The Mozza Cookbook, *and other books. She is a four-time winner of the James Beard Award.*

Introduction

The Power of a Good Meal
with Family & Friends

For me, the foundation of cooking always started with family.

When I was a young child, my family was forced to emigrate at the start of the Iranian Revolution. We were among the luckier ones. My father was a partner at a large construction company that built projects for the Iranian government, and he'd heard rumblings that the revolution was near. Without hesitation, he sent my two older brothers to boarding school in Switzerland and then sent my mother and me to London. We had to leave everything behind: our family, our friends, our home, and all of the possessions that my parents had worked so hard to provide for us. Along with so many others, our lives changed dramatically. It was a couple of years before my father was able to leave Iran to be with my mother and me. My brothers rejoined us when we found ourselves safely in Los Angeles, a place where we had neither family nor connections and barely spoke the language. My father was hired as an engineer at Parsons International Engineering in Pasadena, and my mother, who never had worked, desperately tried to find any job she could get to help my father in rebuilding our lives. Eventually they were able to save up enough to buy a small dry-cleaning business in Beverly Hills, one that my mother still runs to this day.

My parents worked endless hours to create a new life for us. As a result, I rarely saw them. In Iran, we had every meal together and spent countless hours around the table filled with family, friends, and conversation. In Los Angeles, we were a family I barely recognized. I was a latchkey kid, often alone while my parents were at work and my brothers, nine and ten years older than me, were busy with their own lives. Instead of watching *Scooby-Doo* like my school friends, I became deeply absorbed in cooking shows, specifically those of Julia Child and Jacques Pépin. When I watched Julia and Jacques cook, I got a tiny taste of that familial warmth that I so missed from my early childhood.

Julia and Jacques weren't my real family, of course, but they gave me an idea. And so at the age of eight, I started cooking for my family, in the hope that sharing that feeling of warmth might spread and maybe even get us around the table together again. I crossed my fingers—and it worked. Even if my parents worked until late in the evening and arrived home too tired to even talk, they were happy to see dinner waiting, proudly prepared by little me. They would join me at the table, and after a warm meal and a couple of words, shake off some of the stress from the day. Seeing their reactions as they took a moment to rest and enjoy these meals brought me so much joy and comfort. We were back together, connecting in the way I'd missed so much.

Ever since this discovery, cooking has been my passion. I never thought, however, that it would lead to my career. After college, I found success in the movie business, but I was always drawn back to my love of food. I threw myself into cooking at home and hosting friends while becoming a loyal customer of some of LA's best restaurants. Finally, in 2011, with the support of my husband, Christian, my father, and some of our closest friends, I put all of our savings into opening our first Olive & Thyme. We gave that little mom-and-pop our all and watched it grow from the blood, sweat, and tears we put into it. Nine years, two children, and two restaurants later, we have created restaurants that connect the community with our passion for real relationships and great food—and the incredible and rewarding experience of blending the two together.

My philosophy behind Olive & Thyme is simple: quality ingredients that are fresh, natural, and local—all put together with love. All of our recipes have been handcrafted from experiences in my life, drawn from family recipes and people who inspire me. At Olive & Thyme, nothing is frozen; everything is made fresh daily. I don't believe in compromising quality for my family, and that principle carries into my restaurant family as well.

In those early years of hosting dinner parties and carrying on my parents' tradition of family Sunday, which always involved good meals, I found myself in the kitchen the entire time. I came to realize that this was defeating the whole point of inviting people into my home: to connect with my guests and help them connect with one another. I had to get more organized so I could actually be present with my friends and family, and I wasn't opposed to reducing the stress of cooking complicated recipes either. I set out to simplify some of my favorite recipes while keeping their essential flavor profiles. I figured out my shortcuts, which I share in these pages. At the heart of this is the reason for all that I do—you have to be present, or what's the point?

I've always believed that no matter what you do in life, good food, wine, and music can make you a family. It's a myth that making beautiful food and entertaining with style has to be complicated, expensive, and stressful. My goal with this book is to inspire you and give you the tools to gather around the table more often with the people you love, share delicious food and wine, listen to great music, and celebrate one another and the simple pleasures of life, whether it's a quick dinner for two or a party for two dozen.

The farmers' market dictates what I cook. I let it inspire what I'm going to make for my family for the week and what to source for the restaurant. It's also a great place where I can teach my children the importance of supporting local farmers and the benefits of eating organic, fresh food.

Introduction

Day

Sunday is my favorite day. Early Sunday mornings mean sleepy kids with wild bedheads, making breakfast together, and watching their latest performances in our kitchen. We take the kids to the farmers' market and teach them about fresh produce and what's in season, picking out whatever is at its peak. I let our market goods determine the menu for the week and start to think about what to make for dinner that evening. My best dishes come from letting the season decide the plate, and I love the philosophy of cooking what is both seasonal and local.

The rest of the day moves slowly and organically, as lunch turns into dinner while family and friends flow in and out of our home. Visitors sit around the table and chat or hang out by the pool watching the kids swim while I spend my time in my kitchen, popping out to talk in between chopping and stirring. This is where I find my true joy—with a glass of wine in my hand and some Tom Petty in the background, my kitchen is my happy place. On a rare occasion, my husband and I get a morning to ourselves, but the theme remains the same. Whatever day it is, this is the quality time that feeds my passion for everything that I do. Special occasions, such as baby showers or birthday parties, can require a bit more structure, but this isn't what I call "work"—this is what fuels me.

Breakfast

Buttermilk Biscuits

There are few things in this world more gluttonous than a homemade buttermilk biscuit. Right out of the oven, they are crisp on the outside, fluffy on the inside, and flake apart as you rip them open to stuff with butter and preserves. There's nothing more satisfying than watching the steam rise out of a fresh biscuit while your butter melts into it!

Makes 10 to 12 biscuits

1½ sticks (12 tablespoons) unsalted butter

3½ cups all-purpose flour (I prefer King Arthur), divided

1 tablespoon kosher salt

1 tablespoon sugar

½ teaspoon baking soda

1 tablespoon baking powder

1¼ cups buttermilk

2 egg yolks

2 tablespoons heavy cream

Preheat the oven to 400°.

Cut butter into 6 2-tablespoon slices and return to the refrigerator to keep cold until needed.

In a large mixing bowl, add 3 cups flour, salt, sugar, baking soda, and baking powder. Whisk together until thoroughly combined.

The remaining steps need to be completed in a timely manner to prevent the butter from getting warm, which is key to having flaky biscuits.

Remove butter from the refrigerator and add the pieces to the flour mixture. Using a pastry cutter, press down and use a slight rocking motion to push the butter into the flour. Continue to cut the butter until the largest pieces of floured butter are nickel size, about 1½ minutes.

Using a wooden spoon, mound the floured butter mixture in the center of the bowl. Slowly add the buttermilk, stirring gently to incorporate, just until it's all blended but no longer; you do not want to overwork the dough.

Sprinkle 3 tablespoons flour onto a cool, nonporous work surface; sprinkle 3 tablespoons flour on your hands to avoid sticking. Lift out all of the dough with your floured hands and place it on the floured work surface. Using your hands, press and mold into an 8-by-8-inch square. Lightly dust the top of the dough with 1 tablespoon flour (to prevent your hands from sticking) and fold the dough over from front to back, leaving you with an 8-by-4-inch rectangle. Fold the dough once again lengthwise, so you have a 4-by-4-inch square.

Sprinkle 1 tablespoon flour onto a rolling pin. Using the floured pin, roll the dough to 1 inch thick. The dough should be an approximate 10-by-10-inch square. Cut out the biscuits with a 2¾-inch cookie cutter. After cutting out 9 biscuits, gently reincorporate remaining dough by molding it into a square and folding it over twice again. Press to 1 inch thick and cut 2 to 3 more biscuits. After all the biscuits are cut, place them on a parchment-lined plate in the freezer for 30 minutes to harden the butter. DO NOT SKIP THIS STEP.

Recipe continues on next page

To make the egg wash, whisk together egg yolks and heavy cream in a small mixing bowl until thoroughly combined. Set aside.

When chilled, remove biscuits from the freezer, place them on a parchment-lined baking sheet, and brush them with the egg wash. Place the sheet on the middle rack of the oven and bake until golden brown, 15 to 20 minutes. Serve warm with Fresh Preserves (recipe follows), honeycomb, and butter.

Fresh Preserves

The best thing about making Fresh Preserves, other than how easy it is, is that you can make them with literally any fruit you want. It doesn't have to just be strawberry! You can use any other berries or stone fruits. I love adding herbs and citrus to mine. I like to make this on a day when I'm home relaxing and not in a rush to be anywhere. While not complicated, preserves take a while to cook and need some attention from time to time.

Makes 3 cups

4 pounds strawberries, stems removed
4 cups granulated sugar
Juice of 1 lemon

1 tablespoon lemon zest
1 sprig fresh rosemary, placed in an herb sachet
1 24-ounce sterile mason jar

Place strawberries, sugar, lemon, and zest in a large saucepan. Set heat to low and bring to a simmer. Simmer for 1 hour, stirring occasionally so the fruit doesn't burn, and then add rosemary in the herb sachet. Cook for another hour, still stirring from time to time. Remove the rosemary sachet and simmer for an additional 40 minutes.

Remove preserves from heat, transfer to mason jar, and set aside to cool before sealing tightly. Store in the refrigerator for up to 1 year.

Granola

Best granola in town, hands down. It's good with milk, on yogurt, on ice cream, or by itself. Not everyone is a big fan of coconut, myself included, but its creaminess really works with this recipe.

Makes 6 cups

1 cup plain cashews
¾ cup shredded coconut
1 cup shaved almonds
1¼ cups old-fashioned oats
¼ cup canola oil

½ cup brown sugar
½ cup 100% maple syrup
½ teaspoon kosher salt
¾ cup dried cherries

Preheat the oven to 250°.

Place cashews, coconut, almonds, and oats in a large bowl and mix gently until thoroughly incorporated.

In a medium mixing bowl, add canola oil, brown sugar, maple syrup, and salt and whisk until thoroughly incorporated. Pour over the dry oat mixture and gently mix with a spatula until coated. Transfer the mix to 2 parchment-lined baking sheets, being careful not to crowd the granola, and bake until golden, 75 to 80 minutes. Check every 20 minutes and stir with a wooden spoon. Remove from oven and set aside to cool.

Once it has cooled, return granola to a large mixing bowl, add the dried cherries, and toss with a wooden spoon. Store in a tightly sealed glass container for up to 2 weeks.

Fruit Parfaits

What I love about fruit parfaits is how versatile they are: perfect for a cup on the go, beach picnics, quick family breakfasts, entertaining, and brunches. Your fruit can be prepped the night before, and the parfaits can be assembled in the morning to save time. They're a real crowd-pleaser—everybody loves parfaits! They offer a beautiful presentation that is easy to put together in no time.

Serves 8

8 6-ounce jars or cups

2½ cups Greek yogurt, divided

1 cup clover honey, divided

1½ cups Granola (recipe on page 23), divided

1 cup blueberries

1 cup raspberries

1 cup blackberries

8 sprigs fresh mint

Add ¼ cup yogurt to each jar or cup. Top each with 2 tablespoons honey, and then add ¼ cup Granola to each. Sprinkle berries on top of the Granola (about 8 berries per jar or cup). Top each with a dollop (about 1 tablespoon) of yogurt, garnish with a mint sprig, and serve.

Oatmeal

This is a perfect example of how to elevate a simple dish into something special. The dried cherries sweeten the oatmeal while adding a touch of bright tartness. If you can't find dried cherries or prefer a little sweetness over tartness, use dried cranberries instead.

Serves 4

3 cups milk

2 cups quick-cooking oats

1 cup dried cherries

1 cup roasted shaved almonds

½ cup dark brown sugar

Place a saucepan over medium-high heat and add milk, bringing it to a light simmer. Turn the flame down to low. With a wooden spoon, stir in the oats. Simmer, stirring occasionally, until thickened, 10 to 12 minutes.

Remove from the heat, add dried cherries and almonds, and stir together gently with a wooden spoon. Transfer to a serving bowl and serve with a side of brown sugar.

Arugula, Bacon & White Cheddar Quiche

A classic quiche is such a great go-to dish. Kids love them, they work well for parties, they make for good leftovers, and you can change out the flavor ingredients however you like. The combination in this recipe is a restaurant favorite, but feel free to experiment, perhaps substituting tomatoes, feta, and spinach. I'm partial to brie and mushroom myself—that's my jam for brunch at home.

It's ideal to make your own crust from scratch, and I have a simple recipe for that on page 163, but that's not always realistic for home cooks who are juggling family, work, and a busy life, so feel 100 percent free to buy a pre-made crust.

Serves 6

1 9-inch pie crust, thawed if frozen (recipe on page 163)

6 large eggs

1½ cups heavy cream

10 to 15 strips bacon, cooked and chopped

1 cup shredded white cheddar

1 cup chopped arugula

Preheat the oven to 350°.

Crack eggs into a medium mixing bowl and whisk them together. Slowly pour in heavy cream and continue to whisk until thoroughly combined. Whisk in chopped bacon, white cheddar, and arugula.

Place the pie crust in its foil pie pan in the middle of a baking sheet and pour mixture into the crust. Carefully place baking sheet on the middle rack in the oven, keeping the quiche as level as possible as you move it.

While the quiche bakes, compose the Arugula Salad (recipe on page 31).

After 45 minutes, remove quiche from the oven and place on a cooling rack or counter to cool. Flip quiche out of its foil pie pan, slice, and serve with Arugula Salad.

Arugula Salad

6 cups baby arugula
¼ cup freshly grated parmesan

½ cup Lemon Dressing (recipe follows)
2 tablespoons Toasted Breadcrumbs (recipe on page 69)

Place arugula and parmesan in a large mixing bowl. Lightly toss together and transfer to a serving dish. Just before serving, add Lemon Dressing and Breadcrumbs to the salad.

LEMON DRESSING

Makes ½ cup

Juice of 2 lemons
¼ cup extra-virgin olive oil

Sea salt and freshly ground black pepper

In a small mixing bowl, combine lemon juice, olive oil, and salt and pepper. Whisk together until fully incorporated.

Smoothies

These are great for when you're on the go. Feel free to change it up—if you don't like pistachios, try another nut, or try kale in place of spinach if you're not a fan.

Strawberry Banana Smoothie

Makes 1 smoothie

1 banana, peeled and broken into pieces

2 apples, cut into quarters

8 frozen strawberries

¾ cup orange juice

1 fresh mint leaf

Place all ingredients in a blender and purée until smooth. Pour into a glass and garnish with a mint leaf.

Blueberry Pistachio Smoothie

Makes 1 smoothie

1 cup fresh blueberries

2 apples, cut into quarters

2 tablespoons shelled pistachios

¾ cup almond milk

½ cup ice

Place all ingredients in a blender and purée until smooth, until there are no signs of pistachio chunks. Pour into a glass and serve.

Green Boost Smoothie

Makes 1 smoothie

2 cups baby spinach

1 celery stick, chopped

1 carrot, chopped

2 apples, cut into quarters

¾ cup almond milk

Place all ingredients in a blender and purée until smooth. Pour into a glass and serve.

Iced Matcha Blast

I don't drink coffee often. I find that matcha gives me that much-needed energy to get through the day without the jitters. It's also packed with antioxidants and other cleansing properties, so you can feel good about your daily fix!

Like your drinks warm? Heat the milk before whisking in the matcha, and skip the ice. And if you don't like it sweet, leave out the honey.

Makes 1 12-ounce drink

1 ounce hot water

1 ounce matcha powder

1 teaspoon honey

10 ounces cold soy or almond milk

1 cup ice

Combine hot water and matcha powder with a small whisk. Once the matcha is fully dissolved, add honey and continue to whisk until combined. Add soy or almond milk and whisk together.

Pour over ice and serve.

Brunch

Avocado & Burrata Toast

In Danish culture, "toasts" are any sort of open-faced sandwich, and they've become a staple at home thanks to my Danish mother-in-law. So, it was a natural for me to serve them when I first opened the restaurant. Today, this toast is the single most popular dish at Olive & Thyme. What really makes it are the heirloom tomatoes—their depth of flavor, acid, and sweetness balance the earthy fat of the sliced avocado. Sea salt and olive oil marinate and brighten the creamy burrata, bringing all the flavors to life.

Serves 2

2 ½-inch-thick slices sourdough bread

1 to 2 heirloom tomatoes

1 avocado

2 teaspoons balsamic vinegar

1 cup burrata cheese

Extra-virgin olive oil

Sea salt and freshly ground black pepper

4 medium basil leaves, cut into a chiffonade

Place a griddle on medium-high heat until hot (it takes 5 to 7 minutes). If you don't have a griddle, a barbecue works great. Toast bread until it has dark brown grill marks, 1 to 2 minutes. Flip and repeat the process. When the bread is grilled, set it on a cooling rack to prevent it from steaming and getting soggy.

Remove cores from the tomatoes, cut into 6 to 8 vertical wedges, and set aside.

To thinly slice and fan the avocado, start by carefully cutting the avocado in half lengthwise by rotating your knife blade around the pit. Hold the avocado in your hands and give a quarter turn to release the pit. Carefully remove the pit and skin. Lay avocado halves vertically on a cutting board pit side down and slice each thinly. To fan a sliced avocado half, gently press on it from left to right.

Place each fanned avocado half on a piece of the toasted bread. Top with tomato wedges and drizzle 1 teaspoon balsamic over each. Arrange ½ cup burrata over the tomatoes on each toast. Drizzle olive oil to taste over the burrata and garnish with salt, pepper, and basil.

Smoked Salmon Toast

A perfect dish for brunch, this plates beautifully with bright colors and fresh sprigs of dill. Crème fraîche offers a light and tangy alternative to often-pastier cream cheese.

Serves 2

2 ½-inch-thick slices sourdough bread

6 tablespoons crème fraîche

6 ounces smoked salmon

1 whole avocado, thinly sliced

2 hard-boiled eggs, thinly sliced

12 Thyme Pickled Radishes (recipe follows), thinly sliced

1 tablespoon capers

2 sprigs fresh dill

Place a griddle on medium-high heat until hot, 5 to 7 minutes. If you don't have a griddle, a barbecue works great. Toast bread until it has dark brown grill marks, 1 to 2 minutes. Flip and repeat the process. When the bread is grilled, set it on a rack to prevent it from steaming and getting soggy.

Spread half the crème fraîche across each piece of toast. Layer smoked salmon on the crème fraîche. Fan the thinly sliced avocado and lay it atop the salmon. Top avocado with sliced egg, Thyme Pickled Radishes, and capers. Garnish with fresh dill. Transfer to plate and enjoy immediately.

Thyme Pickled Radishes

Preserve your produce before it goes to waste. You can basically pickle anything! This recipe is for radishes; try it with carrots, onions, turnips, or any number of vegetables.

Makes 1 24-ounce jar

2 cups red wine vinegar

2 cups apple cider vinegar

1 tablespoon sugar

1 24-ounce sterile mason jar

8 sprigs fresh thyme

1 big bunch radishes, skin on, washed well, and thinly sliced

1 teaspoon kosher salt

Place vinegars and sugar in a small saucepan. Over medium flame, bring to a boil, stirring occasionally. Remove from heat and set aside.

While waiting for the vinegars to boil, add to the mason jar 2 sprigs of thyme, then layer some radish slices. Add 2 more sprigs of thyme, and layer with more radishes. Continue this process until you're out of thyme and radishes. Sprinkle salt on the top of the radishes and thyme, then pour all the hot liquid into the jar. Seal and set aside to cool at room temperature, then gently shake to incorporate the ingredients. Set aside in a room-temperature spot to pickle for 2 to 3 days. Once the jar is opened, refrigerate it.

MELINA'S HACK

If you like a little extra kick to your pickles, add a split chile pepper. You can also add any of your favorite fresh herbs as well as a bay leaf or, perhaps, some mustard seeds. Feel free to experiment—what do you have in your pantry?

Shakshuka

This classic is one of my go-to brunch dishes, because it has so many flavor profiles. I love the richness and sweetness of the tomatoes, and their acid works so well with the sumac and spices. With the addition of the creaminess of the feta, this dish reminds me of all of the cultures I love to put together.

Serves 4 to 6

1 tablespoon extra-virgin olive oil

1 onion, diced

3 cloves garlic, chopped

2 medium yellow or orange bell peppers, seeded and chopped (avoid green peppers)

3 ripe tomatoes, diced

4 ounces double-concentrated tomato paste (I prefer Mutti)

1 can crushed tomatoes

2 tablespoons paprika

3 teaspoons ground cumin

3 teaspoons chili powder

3 teaspoons sea salt

1 teaspoon sumac

¼ teaspoon garlic powder

6 eggs

¼ cup feta crumbles (optional)

⅓ cup chopped Italian parsley

Heat olive oil in a cast-iron skillet over medium heat. Add onion and cook until translucent, 3 to 4 minutes, stirring frequently. Add garlic and sauté, stirring continuously, until aromatic, about 1 minute. Add peppers and sauté, stirring frequently, until softened, 5 to 7 minutes. Add diced tomatoes and simmer 2 minutes. Stir in tomato paste and crushed tomatoes and simmer 5 to 7 minutes.

In a small bowl, mix paprika, cumin, chili powder, sea salt, sumac, and garlic powder. Add spice mixture to skillet, reduce heat to low, and simmer for 15 to 20 minutes—the longer you cook, the better!

Crack 6 eggs around the sides of the skillet. Cover until cooked to taste, 3 to 5 minutes.

Sprinkle with feta and parsley and serve right out of the skillet.

MELINA'S HACK

If you're hosting vegans, remove some of the sauce before dropping in the eggs and cheese and add it to pasta, or serve with just a side of toasted bread.

Simple, Perfect Bread

Making bread for the first time is always intimidating. I hope this recipe will show you that anyone can make it! It's especially fun to make with kids. The hardest part is remembering to start the day before, because the dough has to sit out overnight. Trust me, this simple homemade loaf will taste better than any store-bought bread out there.

Makes 1 loaf

3 cups flour (I prefer King Arthur), plus more
1½ teaspoons kosher salt

½ teaspoon yeast
1⅓ cups water

Add flour, salt, and yeast to a medium mixing bowl and mix with a wooden spoon until combined, 30 to 45 seconds.

Using your hands, mound the flour mixture in the center of the bowl and slowly add water, mixing gently until it all comes together into a loose ball. This will take 2 to 2½ minutes. It should have a sticky consistency.

Transfer dough to a clean bowl. Cover airtight with plastic wrap and set aside on the counter in a cool place overnight so the dough can rise.

The next day, preheat the oven to 475°.

Flour the bottom of a Dutch oven. Flour a nonporous work surface and coat your hands with flour. Remove dough with floured hands and place on the floured work surface. Lightly mold dough into a round shape with your hands (it doesn't need to be perfect). Place dough in Dutch oven. Make 3 to 4 snips with scissors in the top of the dough and dust the top with flour. Put lid on the Dutch oven and place it on the middle rack in the oven toward the back. Bake bread until golden brown and crunchy, about 55 minutes. To check if it's done, the knife or toothpick test should do the trick: Pierce the middle of the loaf with a knife or toothpick—if it comes out clean, it's finished.

Remove bread from the Dutch oven carefully, let cool for about 5 minutes, and serve.

MELINA'S HACK

Want your bread to be less dense? Simply activate the yeast before using it. In a small bowl, whisk together yeast and 1 tablespoon warm water, then add it to the flour mixture.

Watermelon Gazpacho

Gazpacho is in my refrigerator all summer long. It's fast, chilly, and filling, and this variation is a favorite of mine. Cool watermelon is so refreshing and lightly tart, and this recipe gives it a salty and savory twist so it's not too sweet. Gazpacho gets better after a day or two in the fridge, so don't toss this one out!

Makes 8 cups

1 5- to 6-pound watermelon, skinned and cut into a small dice

1 cup diced roma tomatoes

¾ cup (about 2 stalks) diced celery

1 cup diced cucumber

¼ cup diced red onion

½ cup fresh mint leaves, plus more

½ cup granulated sugar

½ cup fresh lemon juice

1 tablespoon Tajín seasoning, plus more

1 teaspoon kosher salt

Put aside 1 cup of the watermelon in the refrigerator. In a Vitamix or blender, add remaining watermelon, tomatoes, celery, cucumber, onion, and mint and blend until almost puréed.

Transfer to a mixing bowl and add sugar, lemon juice, Tajín, and salt and stir together. Refrigerate for 1 hour. When ready to serve, gently stir in the remaining watermelon. Divide into 8 serving bowls and garnish each with a mint leaf and a small sprinkle of Tajín.

NOTE: If you don't have a Vitamix and are using a regular blender, you might need to make this in 2 batches.

NOTE: Tajín is a Mexican seasoning powder made of red chiles, lime, and salt, and it's available at many supermarkets and online.

Crêpes

This recipe has a special place in my heart. My Danish mother-in-law, Vita, used to cook this for me as a treat for breakfast. (To be honest, it's how she won my heart.) She'd save the leftovers for an after-dinner dessert, warm them up, and fill them with vanilla ice cream. I continued this tradition and see the same happiness on my children's faces. I hope they do the same for their children. That's the thing about food—it becomes a legacy.

Makes 6 to 7 crêpes

3 eggs
1 cup whole milk
1 cup all-purpose flour (I prefer King Arthur)
1 tablespoon unsalted butter per crêpe

Edible flowers (optional)
Juice of 1 lemon
½ cup confectioners' sugar

In a large mixing bowl, whisk eggs and milk together. Slowly whisk in flour. Let the batter rest for 15 minutes.

On low-medium heat, melt 1 tablespoon butter in a 6-inch frying pan, making sure the butter coats the bottom of the pan. Hold the pan above the flame 4 to 6 inches and pour about 4 tablespoons batter into the pan. Rotate the pan in a circular motion to cover the entire bottom with batter. Return to the stovetop. If you're using edible flowers, quickly add 2 to 3 of them to the top of the batter (the batter MUST be wet). Cook until the crêpe becomes more solid and the edges become golden brown, 1 to 2 minutes. Using a spatula, flip crêpe onto the flower side and cook for no more than 1 minute—any longer than that, the flowers will brown and shrivel. Place crêpe on a serving plate and keep covered. Continue the process until batter is used up.

Garnish crêpes with a drizzle of lemon juice and dust with confectioners' sugar. Serve immediately.

MELINA'S HACK

To make a crispy, brown, buttery edge, add ¼ teaspoon butter to the sides of the pan before flipping each crêpe.

Stone Fruit & Tomato Salad

For me, summertime means days spent lounging in the backyard, chilled rosé, and lots of stone fruit. This mix of sweet stone fruit and acidic tomatoes topped with cool ricotta and refreshing basil is a delicious and light dish for warm weather. Don't let the complexity of the flavors fool you—there's a real simplicity to this dish. And as a plus, you won't break a sweat while making it.

NOTE: If you can't find pluots or apricots, it's okay to sub in other stone fruits. Use what is seasonal and ripe!

Serves 6

¼ cup pine nuts

6 medium peaches

4 medium nectarines

4 pluots

4 apricots

4 plums

12 heirloom cherry tomatoes, cut in half

¼ cup extra-virgin olive oil, plus more

Sea salt

½ cup chopped basil

1 cup Whipped Ricotta with Basil (recipe follows)

A few baby basil leaves

Preheat the oven to 300°.

Roast pine nuts on a medium baking sheet until golden brown, 5 to 7 minutes, then set aside to cool.

Cut all the stone fruit in wedges and place in a large salad bowl. Add cherry tomatoes, olive oil, salt, and basil and toss together.

Top with Whipped Ricotta, then garnish with roasted pine nuts, basil leaves, a drizzle of olive oil, and a sprinkle of sea salt.

Whipped Ricotta with Basil

Makes 1 cup

1 cup whole milk ricotta cheese

¼ cup fresh basil

Sea salt and freshly ground pepper

1 tablespoon extra-virgin olive oil

Combine ricotta, basil, salt, and pepper in a food processor. Slowly incorporate the olive oil, mixing for 1 to 2 minutes on low speed. Chill and store in the refrigerator for up to 3 days.

Beet Hummus & Avocado Toast

A beautiful dish that's easy to put together, this is built around a savory hummus that's vibrant and satisfying.

Serves 2

2 ½-inch-thick slices sourdough bread
1 cup Beet Hummus (recipe follows)
1 avocado
¼ cup crumbled feta cheese

Extra-virgin olive oil
Sea salt
Fresh basil leaves, cut into chiffonade
Chamomile flowers (optional)

Place a griddle on medium-high heat until hot, 5 to 7 minutes. If you don't have a griddle, a barbecue works great. Toast bread until it has dark brown grill marks, 1 to 2 minutes. Flip and repeat the process. When bread is grilled, set it on a cooling rack to prevent it from steaming and getting soggy.

Spread Beet Hummus evenly, covering each slice of toast.

Carefully cut your avocado in half lengthwise by rotating your knife blade around the pit. Hold the avocado in your hands and give a quarter turn to release the pit. Carefully remove the pit and skin. Lay the avocado half vertically on the cutting board pit side down and slice thinly. To fan the avocado, gently press on the sliced avocado from left to right. Repeat with the other avocado half. Place each fanned avocado half on toasted bread.

Sprinkle feta over the avocados. Drizzle extra-virgin olive oil over the toast and top with sea salt, basil, and chamomile flowers.

BEET HUMMUS

You can make this delicious souped-up hummus in advance; it will keep in the refrigerator for up to 4 days.

Makes 2 cups

1 small red beet
1 medium golden beet
2 tablespoons extra-virgin olive oil, divided
Sea salt

1 tablespoon fresh lemon juice
1 cup Olive & Thyme's Famous Hummus (recipe on page 208)

Preheat the oven to 400°.

Cut the tops off the beets, leaving 1 inch intact. Wash and remove any debris with a damp kitchen towel. Coat beets with 1 tablespoon olive oil and sprinkle with salt. Wrap each beet tightly in foil, place on a baking sheet, and roast until fork-tender, 40 to 45 minutes. When cool enough to touch, cut the ends off, peel, and roughly chop the beets.

Add cooled beets, 1 tablespoon olive oil, and lemon juice to a food processor and blend until smooth, 2 to 3 minutes. Add hummus and continue to process together until fully blended. Taste and add salt as needed. Serve with warmed naan bread or fresh crudités.

Lemony Potato Salad

Have I mentioned that I love lemons? This nontraditional potato salad is bright, complex in flavor, and a little crunchy. Great for picnics and barbecues, it travels well and can be made the night before. In fact, it's better when it's made ahead because the flavors blend a little more. Just make sure to give it a quick stir before serving.

Serves 6 to 8

5 pounds red potatoes, scrubbed, with skin on
1¼ cups diced celery, divided
1 cup chopped scallions, divided
½ cup Best Foods mayonnaise
1 cup sour cream

½ cup fresh lemon juice
2 tablespoons lemon zest
2 tablespoons red wine vinegar
Sea salt and freshly ground pepper

Fill a large pot with water and a pinch of salt. Add potatoes, bring the water to a boil over high heat, and cook potatoes until cooked through, 15 to 20 minutes. When they're done, a fork should easily pierce through them. Drain potatoes and set aside to cool. When cool enough to handle, cut into ¼-inch pieces.

In a large mixing bowl, combine 1 cup celery, ¾ cup scallions, and potatoes.

In a separate mixing bowl, stir together mayonnaise, sour cream, lemon juice, lemon zest, red wine vinegar, salt, and pepper. Add to potato mixture and lightly toss, just until potatoes are fully coated but no longer. Overmixing will cause the potatoes to fall apart and become starchy.

Transfer to a serving bowl, garnish with remaining celery and scallions, add salt and pepper to taste, and serve.

Lunch

Egg Salad Toast

A perfect egg to me is gorgeously soft-boiled and a little gooey in the center. This tiny distinction between soft- and hard-boiled is what has made this toast such a success at the restaurant. When you combine them, you get a beautiful, creamy texture while using way less mayonnaise than a typical egg salad. Overcooking eggs makes them rubbery and gives the yolks a blue or gray tint, but cooking them soft keeps yolks vibrant yellow for an egg salad unlike any you've seen. Chopped dill brings the flavors together while adding a slight contrast in color.

Serves 5

1 tablespoon sea salt

1 tablespoon white vinegar

12 eggs, room temperature

1 tablespoon Dijon mustard

1 cup **Best Foods mayonnaise**

2 tablespoons minced fresh dill, divided

Sea salt and freshly ground pepper

5 slices olive or sourdough bread

½ cup thinly sliced red onions

Add salt and vinegar to a large pot of water and bring to a boil over high heat. Use a slotted spoon to gently lower in the eggs. After 6 minutes, remove 6 of the eggs and drop them immediately into an ice bath. After 4 more minutes, remove the remaining 6 eggs and drop them immediately into an ice bath. Once cooled, peel the shells, roughly chop the eggs, and transfer them to a large mixing bowl.

Add mustard, mayonnaise, and 1 tablespoon dill. Stir gently to combine and add salt and pepper to taste. Set aside while you toast the bread.

Place a griddle on medium-high heat until hot, 5 to 7 minutes. If you don't have a griddle, a barbecue works great. Toast bread until it has dark brown grill marks, 1 to 2 minutes. Flip and repeat the process. Set bread on a cooling rack to prevent it from steaming and getting soggy.

Scatter a few onion slices on a piece of toasted bread and generously mound the egg salad on top. Repeat with the remaining toasts. Garnish with remaining dill and serve immediately.

MELINA'S HACK

Make sure your eggs are at room temperature before cooking them to help prevent them from breaking in the water.

BAT Sandwich

A modern twist on the traditional BLT, this is one of my favorite go-tos. What's better than crunchy bacon coupled with creamy avocado and juicy heirloom tomatoes? If the bacon alone leaves you wanting more protein, add some freshly sliced chicken breast—or if you want to be really adventurous, quickly fry up some slices of bologna.

Makes 1 sandwich

2 slices sourdough bread

2 tablespoons Best Foods mayonnaise

½ avocado, thinly sliced

1 heirloom tomato, sliced

Sea salt and freshly ground pepper

4 to 5 slices Candied Bacon (recipe on page 95)

Place a griddle on medium-high heat until hot, 5 to 7 minutes. If you don't have a griddle, a barbecue works great. Toast bread until it has dark brown grill marks, 1 to 2 minutes. Flip and repeat the process. When the bread is grilled, set it on a cooling rack to prevent it from steaming and getting soggy.

Spread mayonnaise on both pieces of bread. Fan the avocado slices, layer with heirloom tomato dusted with salt and pepper, and then add Candied Bacon. Top with remaining toasted bread, slice sandwich diagonally, and serve.

Lemon Turkey Sandwich

I put lemon on everything, in what some might call excessive amounts. One of my favorite ways to eat lemons is preserved. I came across the idea of combining preserved lemons and sliced turkey, and what a difference it made! The acid adds an entirely new depth of flavor to the sandwich experience. Even store-bought turkey becomes more appealing with the addition of lemons. Once I discovered this great partnership, I never looked back.

Makes 1 sandwich

2 slices rosemary olive oil bread (sourdough works if rosemary is hard to find)

2 tablespoons Garlic Aioli (recipe follows)

5 slices Preserved Lemons (recipe on next page)

1 teaspoon chopped parsley

4 ounces thinly sliced turkey

1 cup baby arugula

1 teaspoon extra-virgin olive oil

2 teaspoons freshly squeezed lemon juice

Sea salt and freshly ground black pepper

Place a griddle on medium-high heat until hot, 5 to 7 minutes. If you don't have a griddle, a barbecue works great. Toast bread until it has dark brown grill marks (1 to 2 minutes), and then flip and grill on the other side. When the bread is grilled, set it on a cooling rack to prevent it from steaming and getting soggy.

Spread Garlic Aioli evenly across the 2 toasted bread slices. Evenly distribute lemon slices on top of one piece of bread and top with parsley. Loosely roll the turkey and set it atop the lemons and parsley.

In a small bowl, toss arugula with olive oil, lemon juice, salt, and pepper. Arrange this arugula mixture on top of the turkey. Top with the remaining slice of bread. Slice sandwich diagonally, serve, and enjoy.

GARLIC AIOLI

Makes 2 cups

1 whole bulb garlic

2 teaspoons extra-virgin olive oil

Heavy pinch sea salt, plus more as needed

2 cups Best Foods mayonnaise

½ teaspoon soy sauce

2 teaspoons lemon zest

1 tablespoon fresh lemon juice

Preheat the oven to 350°.

Cut garlic bulb in half crosswise, so each clove is cut in half. Set halves, cut side up, on a baking sheet and drizzle with olive oil and salt. Roast until golden brown, about 30 minutes. Remove from the oven and set aside to cool.

Once it has cooled, squeeze garlic pieces out of their shells. In the bowl of a food processor, add garlic, mayonnaise, soy sauce, lemon zest, and lemon juice. Process until it has a smooth consistency. Taste and add sea salt if needed. It will keep in the fridge for up to 1 week.

Preserved Lemons

I have so many lemon trees at home, and I hate letting food go to waste, so I started preserving them and experimenting with what they taste good in. When you preserve lemons, they gain a certain tartness and lose a certain sourness, and the peels become softer and more edible. This version has a little chile heat to it.

Makes 4 cups

1 32-ounce sterile mason jar
6 medium lemons
4 cups fresh lemon juice

¼ cup kosher salt
4 chiles de árbol

Wash lemons and remove any debris with a damp kitchen towel. Cut ½ inch off the tops and bottoms of each. Cut each into thin slices (8 to 10 slices per lemon) and remove seeds.

In a medium saucepan, add lemon juice and bring to a boil.

Place 1 tablespoon kosher salt at the bottom of the mason jar, add 2 chiles, and then add 5 to 6 lemon slices. Add more salt on top of the lemons. Continue the process of layering lemon slices and salt until the lemons are used up, leaving 2 to 3 inches of space from the top of the jar.

Pour hot lemon juice over lemons and add remaining chiles, leaving about an inch of space at the top. Seal jar and allow to cool. Once it's cooled a little, shake it to incorporate the ingredients. Let jar sit at room temperature for 2 weeks before using, and if possible, give the jar a shake every day. Once opened, lemons will keep in the refrigerator for up to 2 weeks.

Steak Salad

I make this salad when I'm having people over and don't want to spend a ton of time in the kitchen. It does involve a decent amount of prep, but if you make the components ahead of time, all that's left to do when your guests arrive is compose!

NOTE: If you need help cooking a steak, refer to the Bone-in Ribeye Steak recipe on page 113; you can use the same technique.

Serves 4 to 6

5 cups chopped romaine lettuce

3 cups baby arugula

½ cup blue cheese crumbles

½ cup Caramelized Balsamic Onions (recipe on next page)

¾ cup Sautéed Mushrooms (recipe on next page)

Grainy Mustard Vinaigrette (recipe on next page)

Sea salt and freshly ground pepper

2 pounds steak (New York, Bone-in Ribeye [recipe on page 113], or filet mignon), grilled in advance and chilled

1½ cups Hand-Torn Croutons (recipe on page 69)

In a large bowl, combine the romaine, arugula, most of the blue cheese (reserve a little), Caramelized Balsamic Onions, and Sautéed Mushrooms. Toss lightly with some of the Grainy Mustard Vinaigrette and salt and pepper to taste. Transfer to a serving platter.

Slice cooked steak thinly on a diagonal, against the grain. Arrange atop the salad and garnish with remaining blue cheese and Hand-Torn Croutons. Drizzle with a little more dressing and serve.

Caramelized Balsamic Onions

2 tablespoons butter

2 red onions, sliced

Pinch sea salt

3 tablespoons balsamic vinegar

Heat a medium skillet over medium-high heat. When hot, add butter, onions, and a dash of salt and sauté until onions are translucent, 8 to 10 minutes.

Add balsamic vinegar and continue to sauté until more caramelized, 5 to 8 minutes. Transfer onions to a plate, laying them flat, and allow to cool.

Sautéed Mushrooms

3 tablespoons extra-virgin olive oil

16 ounces brown mushrooms, sliced

3 cloves garlic, minced

Heat olive oil in a saucepan on medium-high heat. Add mushrooms and garlic and sauté, stirring occasionally, until mushrooms are a rich golden brown in color, 15 to 20 minutes.

Grainy Mustard Vinaigrette

I came up with this while having one of my "what's in my pantry?" moments, which have led to some of my best recipes. I wanted my daughter to try something other than her favorite Caesar dressing on every salad, and I thought this would be a healthy and easy option that she'd like—and she did. It's a perfect mix of tangy from the mustards, acid from the lemons, sweetness from the honey, and a little bit bitter from the vinegar. Try saying that ten times fast!

Makes ½ cup

1 tablespoon grainy mustard

1 tablespoon Dijon mustard

⅔ cup extra-virgin olive oil

¼ cup rice wine vinegar

2 teaspoons honey

Juice of 1 lemon

1 tablespoon shallot, diced

Sea salt and freshly ground pepper

In a food processor, add mustards, olive oil, vinegar, honey, lemon juice, and shallot. Process until dressing begins to thicken, 2 to 3 minutes. Add salt and pepper to taste.

Refrigerate for 15 minutes before serving.

Hand-Torn Croutons

Nothing beats a fresh baguette, but I hate it when we don't finish it before it gets stale and I have to toss it. Instead, I started making these easy croutons. They have a longer shelf life after toasting, and they add the perfect crunch to any salad.

Makes 6 cups

1 day-old baguette
4 sprigs fresh thyme, chopped
2 cloves garlic, minced

½ cup extra-virgin olive oil
Sea salt and freshly ground pepper

Preheat the oven to 350°.

Tear 1-inch pieces of bread off the baguette. It doesn't need to be perfect—you want it to have an organic feel.

Place thyme, garlic, olive oil, salt, and pepper in a medium bowl and stir to mix. Add the torn bread and toss with your hands to fully coat with the oil mixture.

Lay torn bread on a large baking sheet, making sure to spread the pieces evenly across the sheet. Bake for 6 minutes, rotate the pan, and bake until golden brown, about another 4 minutes. Remove from the oven and set aside to cool to room temperature before using.

TO MAKE TOASTED BREADCRUMBS

Place croutons in a food processor and pulse until the breadcrumbs are the size you like.

Cobb Salad

I love a good Cobb salad, especially when it's done right. Crisp, light lettuce, crunchy bacon, tender chicken, ripe avocados, perfectly cooked eggs, and just the right amount of blue cheese—what's not to love? My secret ingredient that makes this salad one of the most popular items at Olive & Thyme is the Spicy Russian Dressing. It adds just the right amount of spiciness that makes you want to keep eating until every bite is gone.

Serves 2

2 cups chopped iceberg lettuce

2 cups chopped romaine lettuce

½ cup chopped cooked bacon

1 avocado, chopped

1 cup chopped Roasted Chicken (recipe on page 109)

½ cup crumbled blue cheese

2 hard-boiled eggs, chopped

1 cup halved cherry heirloom tomatoes

Spicy Russian Dressing (recipe follows)

Toss iceberg and romaine in a medium mixing bowl to combine, and evenly distribute the greens into 2 serving bowls.

With the remaining ingredients, start on one side of the bowl and begin with laying down in a thin line the bacon (¼ cup per bowl), followed by avocado (½ avocado per bowl), Roasted Chicken (½ cup per bowl), blue cheese (¼ cup per bowl), egg (1 egg per bowl), and heirloom cherry tomatoes (½ cup per bowl). Place Spicy Russian Dressing on the side and serve.

If you prefer a tossed salad to a composed one, put all the ingredients into a mixing bowl, toss together, and serve with the dressing on the side, as the salad can get soggy quickly.

SPICY RUSSIAN DRESSING

Thousand Island is one of my guilty pleasures: on a salad, on a burger, or simply to dip my fries in. I also like a spicy sauce that leaves my taste buds tingling. This is the perfect blend of both—creamy like a Thousand Island, with just the right amount of heat from the Sriracha.

Makes 4 cups

¼ cup diced white onion

4 medium garlic cloves, peeled

½ cup ketchup

¾ cup Sriracha hot sauce

3½ tablespoons Worcestershire sauce

2½ tablespoons horseradish

2½ cups Best Foods mayonnaise

Sea salt and freshly ground pepper

In a food processor, add onion, garlic, ketchup, Sriracha, Worcestershire, and horseradish. Process until smooth, 2 to 3 minutes. Transfer to a large mixing bowl. Add mayonnaise, a pinch of salt, and a grinding of pepper and whisk thoroughly.

Refrigerate for about 1 hour before serving.

Chopped Salad

This bright and versatile salad is a perfect side to your richest dishes, or, with some added protein, it can be a meal on its own. The pepperoncini and the fresh oregano dressing create a perfect blend of flavors. If you love olives, you'll be a fan of this tart, herbaceous vinaigrette. If you aren't a fan, simply switch it out for the Grainy Mustard Vinaigrette on page 68. For a vegan guest, just leave out the parmesan and you're set.

Serves 6

6 cups chopped romaine lettuce

6 cups chopped iceberg lettuce

2 cups diced tomatoes

2 cups diced celery

1¾ cups garbanzo beans, drained

1 cup chopped Italian parsley

½ cup chopped scallions

1 cup finely chopped pepperoncini

1 cup chiffonade of basil

1½ cups shredded parmesan, divided

Oregano Vinaigrette (recipe follows)

Sliced grilled chicken breast, salami, or other favorite protein (optional)

In a large mixing bowl, combine romaine and iceberg. Add tomatoes, celery, garbanzo beans, parsley, scallions, pepperoncini, basil, and 1 cup parmesan. Lightly toss to combine.

Pour in Oregano Vinaigrette and toss to coat. Top with the protein of your choice and the remaining parmesan, then serve.

OREGANO VINAIGRETTE

Makes 2½ cups

1 cup red wine vinegar

½ cup fresh lemon juice

5 cloves minced garlic

¼ cup dried oregano

1½ cups minced green olives

1 cup extra-virgin olive oil

Combine vinegar, lemon juice, garlic, oregano, and olives in a food processor. Begin to blend the ingredients together and slowly add olive oil. Process for 1 to 2 minutes. Small bits of olives and oregano will still remain.

Store in the refrigerator in a sealed container for up to 1 week.

Curry Chicken Salad

Part of my Sunday ritual is roasting a chicken; I can make so many meals from just one bird. It can be a full entrée on its own, it can be used for a quick sandwich, or it can go into this amazing salad. You can keep the salad in your fridge for your family to snack on with a warmed piece of pita bread, or on a bed of greens, and the recipe is easy like Sunday morning. Most chicken salads call for grapes, but I find their texture a little too mushy, so I prefer to use Granny Smith apples for a crisper crunch.

Serves 6

1 cup Best Foods mayonnaise

¼ cup honey

¼ cup fresh lemon juice

½ cup finely ground curry powder (I prefer Madras)

1 Roasted Chicken, shredded (recipe on page 109)

2 cups peeled and chopped Granny Smith apples

½ cup green raisins

Sea salt and freshly ground pepper

In a medium mixing bowl, add mayonnaise, honey, lemon juice, and curry powder. Whisk together thoroughly.

In a separate large mixing bowl, add Roasted Chicken, apples, and raisins and toss to combine. Add curry mixture and stir together until chicken is fully coated. Add salt and pepper to taste. Serve in a bowl with a side of warmed pita bread or fresh bread.

Spicy Chicken Bowtie Pasta

This is hands down the most popular pasta salad at the restaurant. It became a quick customer favorite with its buttery bowtie pasta, the chunks of feta, and the perfectly spicy and creamy Spicy Russian Dressing. I love to make this when my family heads over to the park for a lunch picnic or to a friend's house for a potluck. It holds up well, and the longer it sits, the better it gets!

Serves 6 to 8

1 pound dry bowtie pasta
Breast meat of 1 Roasted Chicken, shredded and chilled (recipe on page 109)
¾ cup crumbled feta cheese

¾ cup chopped cilantro
¾ cup chopped scallions
2 cups Spicy Russian Dressing (recipe on page 71)
Sea salt

Bring water to a boil over high heat. Add pasta and a pinch of salt. Cook until al dente, about 9 minutes. Drain, saving ½ cup of the pasta water. Set pasta aside to cool.

Once pasta is cooled and dried, place it in a large mixing bowl. Add Roasted Chicken and most of the feta, cilantro, and scallions and toss together. Slowly incorporate Spicy Russian Dressing until the ingredients are fully coated. Garnish with remaining feta cheese, cilantro, and scallions. Taste and add salt if needed.

MELINA'S HACK

Is your pasta sticking together? Sprinkle it with 1 tablespoon of the saved pasta water and lightly toss—the pasta should begin to loosen immediately.

Farro with Roasted Red & Golden Beets

Farro is one of my favorite grains—it has a nutty taste, and it's hearty, healthy, and super filling. The bitterness of the red beets and sweetness of the golden beets elevate the flavor with little fuss.

If you prepare this dish in advance (which you can!), make a little extra dressing, as farro soaks up moist ingredients quickly. Just before serving, drizzle with a little extra dressing and give the salad a light toss.

Makes 4 cups

1 cup dried farro

1 small red beet, cut into ½-inch dice

2 medium golden beets, cut into ½-inch dice

3 tablespoons extra-virgin olive oil, divided

Sea salt

2 tablespoons balsamic vinegar

½ tablespoon Dijon mustard

Freshly ground pepper

2 teaspoons chopped flat-leaf Italian parsley

Juice of ½ lemon

1 cup baby arugula

¼ cup crumbled goat cheese or feta (optional)

Preheat the oven to 350°.

Place farro and 2 cups cold water in a small bowl and set aside to soak for 1 hour.

While it soaks, cut the tops off the beets, leaving 1 inch of the tops intact. Wash and remove any debris with a damp kitchen towel. Coat beets with 1 tablespoon olive oil and sprinkle with salt. Wrap each beet tightly in foil, place on a baking sheet, and roast until fork-tender, 40 to 45 minutes. When cool enough to touch, cut the ends off, peel the skin, dice, and set aside.

When farro has finished soaking, bring 3 cups water in a large saucepan to boil over high heat. Add drained farro and a pinch of salt and return to a boil. Reduce heat to low, cover with a lid, and simmer until cooked through, 10 to 12 minutes. Remove from heat, drain, and set aside to cool.

In a small mixing bowl, whisk together balsamic vinegar, mustard, remaining 2 tablespoons olive oil, and pepper. Slowly pour this balsamic mix into the farro in the pan, tossing it to combine the dressing with the grains. Once fully combined, add diced beets, parsley, lemon juice, arugula, and cheese (or leave the cheese out for a vegan version). Stir to gently combine, taste, and add salt if needed.

Italian White Bean Salad

I've never understood why people use canned beans. Beans are so easy to cook, they're delicious, and they're so versatile. You just have to remember to soak them in water the night before.

I am absolutely obsessed with this salad. It originated from a dish of white beans with onion, parsley, lemon, and olive oil, which has long been a staple at my brunches; I also purée it to put atop crostini for twilight-hour appetizers. This salad is another one of those "what's in your pantry?" discoveries. One day, a few friends stayed over unexpectedly for lunch. I had the white beans already made in the fridge, so I threw together a few other ingredients, added the oil-packed tuna, and fell in love with my own last-minute creation.

Serves 6 to 10

16 ounces dry cannellini white beans, soaked
   overnight
1 large onion, quartered
1 small bunch fresh rosemary
½ cup extra-virgin olive oil
Juice of 2 large lemons
2 tablespoons rice wine vinegar

1 cup roughly chopped parsley
½ medium onion, cut into medium dice
Sea salt
12 ounces oil-packed tuna
1 basket heirloom cherry tomatoes, cut in half
3 cups baby arugula
¼ cup Toasted Breadcrumbs (recipe on page 69)

Soak the beans overnight. It is important to have the beans completely submerged because they will expand. In the morning, strain and rinse the beans in cold water, then set aside.

Add onion and rosemary to a large saucepan of water and bring to a boil. Add the hydrated white beans to the boiling water, stir with a wooden spoon, return to a boil, and reduce the flame to low. Simmer until beans are soft, with the lid slightly ajar to allow steam to escape, 30 to 40 minutes. As they cook, skim off any starch with a slotted spoon. Drain and rinse the cooked beans with cold water to stop the cooking process. Discard the onion and the rosemary, keeping only the beans.

In a medium mixing bowl, toss together 3 cups cooled beans, olive oil, lemon juice, rice wine vinegar, parsley (reserve a little), onion, and salt to taste.

Drain the tuna and use a fork to lightly flake apart the chunks. In a separate bowl, combine the bean mixture with flaked tuna. Toss in cherry tomatoes and arugula, stirring to fully combine all ingredients.

Transfer to a serving bowl, garnish with remaining chopped parsley and Toasted Breadcrumbs, and serve immediately.

MELINA'S HACK

Save the remaining 3 cups of cooked beans in the fridge...and make it a meal for another day. Add olive oil, fresh lemon juice, rice wine vinegar, chopped parsley, shallots, and sea salt. This makes an amazing side to any entrée! Pack it up and take it to your family's beach day or Sunday picnic.

Raw Corn & Avocado Salad

People are always surprised when I tell them they don't have to cook corn. I really love the texture and sweetness of raw corn, especially in this colorful salad. It travels well, so you can take it on picnics or pack it for lunches. If you're making it in advance, save the avocados and dressing and add both just before serving.

Serves 6

6 ears fresh corn

6 radishes, thinly sliced

1 cup coarsely chopped flat-leaf Italian parsley

1 cup diced red onion

2 cups halved cherry heirloom tomatoes

Lime Jalapeño Dressing (recipe follows)

2 whole avocados, peeled and chopped

Remove corn husks and any remaining hairs. Cutting from the top of each corn cob down, remove raw kernels. Discard the cobs.

In a medium bowl, combine corn, radishes, parsley, onion, and tomatoes. Whisk dressing and pour evenly over the salad, tossing lightly until evenly distributed. Top with avocado and serve immediately.

LIME JALAPEÑO DRESSING

Makes 2 cups

¾ cup fresh lime juice

3 large or 6 small jalapeños, seeded and chopped

3 tablespoons honey

1½ teaspoons cumin

¾ cup extra-virgin olive oil

Heavy pinch sea salt and freshly ground pepper

In a food processor, add lime juice, jalapeños, honey, and cumin. Process together and slowly pour in the olive oil, continuing to process until smooth, 2 to 3 minutes. Taste and add salt and pepper as needed. Store in the refrigerator until ready to use.

Whitefish Tacos

This is literally one of the easiest, no-fuss meals that my guests are always raving about. Sometimes it makes me wonder why I spend so much time on some of my more complicated recipes. I like to use a white, flaky fish for my tacos, but if I don't like what I see at the market, salmon makes a great substitute. If I go with salmon, I whip up a quick aioli. Even people who don't love fish really enjoy these tacos.

Don't be intimidated when you buy fish. If you don't have a local fish market, let your local market know that you want a whitefish that hasn't been previously frozen, if possible. Fish should never have a grayish or yellow tint to it. Most importantly, fish should smell like the ocean but never smell "fishy."

I love to set up a taco bar—they're so fun and they bring people together. Add some margaritas and you are golden.

My necessities for the perfect fish taco bar:

Whitefish (recipe on next page)

Jalapeño Slaw (recipe on page 89)

Raw Corn & Avocado Salad (recipe on page 84)

Chopped onions and cilantro

Charred bell peppers

Lime wedges

Sliced radishes

Sliced avocado

Taco Aioli (see next page)

Corn tortillas

Tortilla chips and salsa

Margaritas (see Watermelon Margaritas, page 225)

MELINA'S HACK

If chopping onions makes you cry, put them in the freezer for 15 minutes first. That will slow down the release of sulfur vapors—that is, the stuff that makes you cry!

Whitefish

The key ingredient for my fish taco bar, this simple fish dish also makes for a tasty, healthy entrée when paired with some veggies or a salad. Try it with the Roasted Cauliflower with Pine Nut Purée (recipe on page 146) for a simple but elegant luncheon or a family dinner.

Serves 4 to 6

3 pounds fresh flaky whitefish, filleted and cleaned
3 lemons
1 teaspoon sea salt, divided

1 teaspoon freshly ground pepper, divided
¼ cup finely chopped fresh parsley, divided
1½ teaspoons extra-virgin olive oil, divided

Preheat the oven to 350°.

In an oven-safe ceramic baking dish, place fish flat in the dish (no overlapping). Top with the juice of 1 lemon, ½ teaspoon salt, ½ teaspoon pepper, and ⅛ cup parsley. Drizzle with ¾ teaspoon olive oil, then flip the fish over and repeat with the juice of another lemon and the remaining salt, pepper, parsley, and oil.

Thinly slice 1 lemon into circles and place 1 slice on each fish fillet.

Place baking dish on the middle rack and roast until cooked through, 12 to 15 minutes. (For a thicker cut like halibut or sea bass, it may take 25 to 30 minutes.)

Once fish is cooked, remove the cooked lemon slices. Transfer fish to a serving platter if you're setting up a taco bar, or plate with a vegetable or salad if it's an entrée.

TACO AIOLI

Put some mayonnaise in a small mixing bowl and add a little Dijon mustard, juice from a lemon, a little finely chopped parsley, salt, and pepper. Stir it up and set it out on your taco bar.

Jalapeño Slaw

This tastes best if you make it at least a half hour in advance for the flavors to combine.

Makes 4 cups

2 cups thinly sliced red cabbage

2 cups thinly sliced green cabbage

¼ cup chopped parsley

1 jalapeño, chopped finely

Juice of 1 lemon

1 tablespoon extra-virgin olive oil

3 tablespoons Best Foods mayonnaise

1½ tablespoons red wine vinegar

1 teaspoon sea salt

Combine cabbages, parsley, and jalapeño in a mixing bowl.

In a separate mixing bowl, whisk together lemon juice, olive oil, mayonnaise, vinegar, and salt. Pour it into the cabbage mixture and lightly toss until the slaw is fully coated.

Cover and store in the refrigerator until ready to serve.

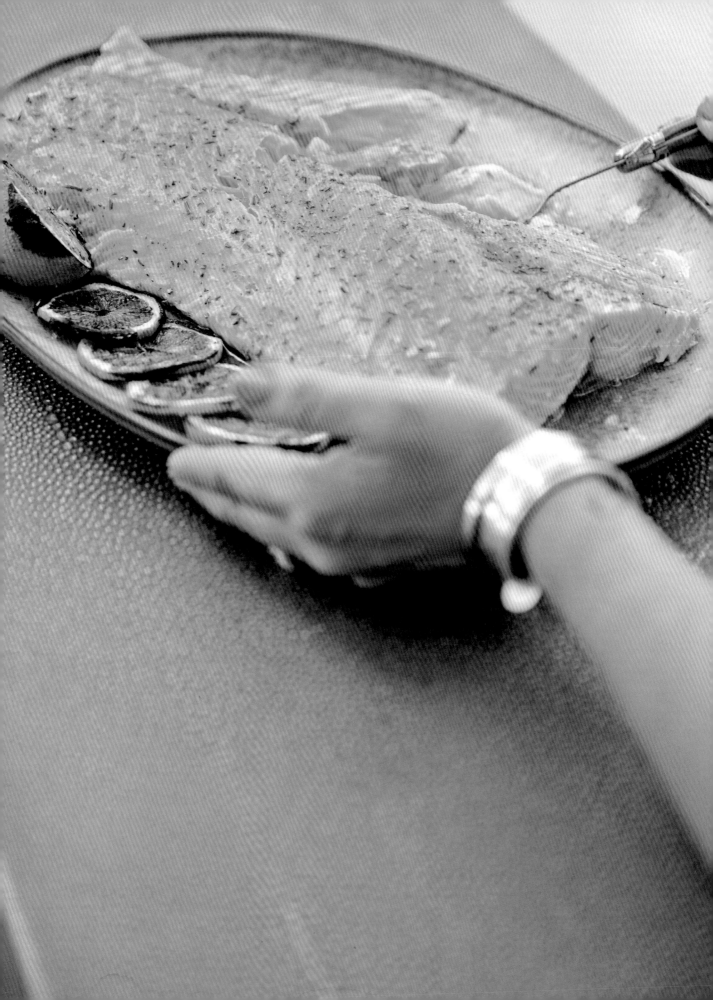

Night

Early evening is the most romantic time of day. The sun is setting, your twinkle lights are on, music is playing, and people are winding down. Whether it's cocktails for two, a celebration with friends, or a cozy night in, it is always a magical time to connect over music, food, and don't forget the wine.

Between cooking complicated meals, plating them artfully, and timing it all correctly, dinners can be daunting. You shouldn't have to be a professional chef to enjoy cooking. The recipes in this section address this challenge. They are easily prepped and can be made ahead of time, reducing any crazy stress and letting you hang with your friends and family, along with that martini you so desperately deserve. Not to mention they make great leftovers, just in case you need to nurse that hangover. Whether it's a dinner party or a dinner at home, here you'll find my favorites for everyday meals, from Sunday suppers like my Roasted Chicken to easy weeknight meals like the three-ingredient Pork Chops with Roasted Vegetables.

Trust me when I say: Turn on your favorite band, pour yourself a glass of wine, and just enjoy the process (I said "a" glass!).

Appetizers

Jalapeño Bacon Deviled Eggs

These deviled eggs are truly evil. They're so rich and decadent that you can really only eat a couple. Or three…or maybe four. We won't judge when you choose to say "when." A perfect bit of sweet and salt from Candied Bacon, coupled with the crunch and heat of fresh jalapeño, puts other deviled eggs to shame.

Makes 24 deviled eggs

2¾ tablespoons white vinegar, divided

12 large eggs, room temperature

1 cup **Best Foods mayonnaise**

2 tablespoons Dijon mustard

1 teaspoon smoked paprika, plus more for garnish

1 tablespoon sea salt, plus more

24 thin slices jalapeño

4 slices Candied Bacon (recipe follows), each cut into 6 pieces

24 chive "batons" (pieces cut into ½-inch lengths)

Extra-virgin olive oil

Bring water to a boil, then add a pinch of salt and 2 tablespoons vinegar. Using a slotted spoon, carefully lower eggs into the water without breaking them and cook for 10 minutes. Remove eggs from hot water and run cold water over them to stop the cooking. Once they are completely cooled, peel the eggs (don't rush the cooling process).

Cut eggs in half vertically, cleaning the knife with a towel after cutting each egg. If any yolk gets stuck on the knife, save it for the filling. When all eggs are halved, carefully separate the yolks and whites.

In a food processor, combine yolks, mayonnaise, remaining ¾ tablespoon vinegar, mustard, paprika, and salt and slowly pulse until smooth. Transfer mix to a piping bag and pipe about 1½ tablespoons of yolk mix into each egg white.

Garnish each deviled egg with a jalapeño slice, Candied Bacon, a chive baton, and a dusting of paprika. Sprinkle with sea salt and a drizzle of olive oil and serve immediately.

CANDIED BACON

Makes 4 slices

2 tablespoons dark brown sugar

¼ cup 100% maple syrup

4 slices bacon

Preheat the oven to 350°.

In a small mixing bowl, stir together brown sugar and maple syrup.

Lay bacon on a wire rack and set the rack onto a parchment-lined baking sheet. Brush bacon with the sugar-syrup mix. Bake until cooked through, 6 to 8 minutes. Set aside to cool before using.

Store in refrigerator in a sealed container for up to 2 days. Always allow Candied Bacon to reach room temperature before using it.

Bacon-Wrapped Dates

A favorite at the restaurant, these babies disappear *fast*. They literally overflow with flavor and gooey-chewy texture, making it nearly impossible to eat just one, and even a "disliking" of blue cheese won't stop you.

Makes 12 dates

12 Medjool dates

6 slices bacon

2 tablespoons creamy blue cheese, like Saint Agur, divided

½ tablespoon clover honey

3 to 4 toasted walnuts, crushed

Preheat the oven to 350°.

Soak dates in hot water for 10 minutes. Pull them out of the water and peel the skin off of each. Using a paring knife, cut a slit lengthwise in each and remove the pits.

Lay bacon slices flat on a baking sheet and bake until partially cooked, about 13 minutes. Remove, cool, and cut each slice in half with cooking scissors.

Stuff each date with ½ teaspoon of blue cheese. Wrap each with ½ piece of par-cooked bacon, place on a baking sheet, and bake for 12 minutes.

Arrange on a serving platter, drizzle with honey, and garnish with toasted walnuts. Serve immediately.

Corn with a Kick

In downtown Los Angeles, there's an incredible street vendor who has the freshest corn cart. He grills corn on the husk right in front of you, melts the butter, and adds lime and chili powder. So simple but such a flavorful dish. This is my take on this street-cart favorite.

Serves 4 to 6

4 ears fresh corn, husks and silks removed
4 tablespoons (½ stick) butter
Juice of 1 lime

Tajín seasoning
Garlic salt
Queso fresco for garnish

Roast, steam, or grill the corn, as you prefer, until it's cooked through. When the cobs are cool enough to handle, hold them vertically and use a sharp knife to cut off the kernels from top to bottom.

Melt butter in a medium saucepan. Add corn kernels and toss to coat. Remove from heat and place in a medium mixing bowl. Add lime juice, Tajîn, and a dash of garlic salt and toss together. Transfer to a serving bowl and garnish with queso fresco.

MELINA'S HACK

This variation works great for when you're entertaining:

Roast, steam, or grill corn on the cob, as you prefer, until it's cooked through. When the cobs are cool enough to handle, hold them horizontally, and with a sharp knife, cut directly through each cob to give yourself 2-inch slices (like in the photo at left).

Melt butter in a medium saucepan. Toss your corn chunks in the butter until coated and remove from the heat. In a medium mixing bowl, add lime juice, Tajín, and a dash of garlic salt and toss together with corn. Line a baking sheet with parchment paper, lay the corn flat, insert bamboo skewers in the middle, transfer to serving platter, and garnish with queso fresco.

Salmon in Butter Lettuce

Bright in both flavor and color, this happy-hour favorite of mine offers yet another great use for those preserved lemons you now have in your kitchen. (Soon you will love lemons as much as I do!) It's filling enough to tide you and your guests over until dinner. The flavor profile also makes it perfect for brunch.

Makes about 18 appetizers

1½ to 2 pounds wild-caught salmon, cleaned and deboned

2 teaspoons Dijon mustard

1 tablespoon extra-virgin olive oil

Juice of 1 lemon

Kosher salt

18 to 20 butter lettuce leaves (can substitute Little Gems)

1½ to 2 cups cooked basmati rice

½ cup Grainy Mustard Vinaigrette (recipe on page 68), divided

18 to 25 slices Preserved Lemons (recipe on page 64)

Chopped flat-leaf Italian parsley for garnish

Dill sprigs for garnish

Sea salt

Preheat the oven to 350°.

Line a baking sheet with parchment paper. Lay salmon on the parchment skin side down. Rub mustard on top of the salmon, drizzle with olive oil and lemon juice, and sprinkle liberally with kosher salt. Roast until flaky and cooked through, 20 to 25 minutes.

In each butter lettuce leaf, place a small palm-size portion of rice. Drizzle each with a little Grainy Mustard Vinaigrette and add 1 or 1½ slices of Precerved Lemons. Sprinkle with parsley and top with a piece of the salmon. Garnish each with a sprig of dill, add sea salt to taste, and serve.

Crostini

Crostini (tiny toasts) are a blank canvas and a perfect vessel for whatever toppings you love. Everyone likes them, and they can easily be made according to the dietary tastes or limitations of each guest. Below and on the next page are a few of my personal favorites, but you can make your own versions if you don't care for figs or tomatoes. Apples and blue cheese with honey are a great option, too!

Fig, Goat Cheese & Thyme Crostini

Makes 10 to 12 toasts

8 ounces goat cheese
4 teaspoons chopped fresh thyme, divided
1 tablespoon extra-virgin olive oil
1 baguette

8 to 10 fresh figs, cut into ¼-inch slices
½ tablespoon clover honey
Sea salt

Preheat the oven to 325°.

In a mixing bowl, combine goat cheese, 2 teaspoons thyme, and olive oil and set aside.

Cut the baguette on the bias into 1-inch slices. Place on a baking sheet and toast in the oven for 5 minutes. Remove and set aside to cool for 2 minutes.

Spread goat cheese mixture on the toast. Top with 3 to 4 fig slices per crostini. Garnish with a drizzle of honey, a sprinkle of thyme, and a dash of sea salt and serve immediately.

More crostini on the next page

Pomodoro & Goat Cheese Crostini

Makes 10 to 12 crostini

1 basket cherry tomatoes, each cut in half
Juice of ½ lemon
Extra-virgin olive oil
1 tablespoon finely chopped shallots

Sea salt and freshly ground pepper
1 baguette
6 tablespoons goat cheese, divided
Micro basil or minced basil for garnish

Preheat the oven to 325°.

In a small bowl, combine tomatoes, lemon juice, a healthy drizzle of olive oil, shallots, salt, and pepper and set aside.

Cut the baguette on the bias into 1-inch slices. Drizzle each piece with olive oil and a little salt. Place on a baking sheet and toast in the oven for 5 minutes. Remove and set aside to cool for 2 minutes.

Spread about ½ tablespoon goat cheese on each crostini. Top with tomato mixture, garnish with basil, and serve.

White Bean Crostini

Makes 10 to 12 crostini

3 cups white beans
1 baguette
¼ cup extra-virgin olive oil, divided, plus a little more
2 cloves garlic, roughly chopped

2 teaspoons finely chopped rosemary
Juice of 1 lemon
¼ cup chopped flat-leaf Italian parsley
Sea salt and freshly ground pepper

Preheat the oven to 325°.

Soak beans overnight. Make sure to completely submerge them, as they will expand. Drain and rinse with cold water.

Bring a large saucepan of water, with a pinch of salt, to a boil. Add beans and return to a boil. Reduce flame to low and simmer until beans are soft, 30 to 40 minutes. Skim off any starch with a slotted spoon. Rinse and set aside to cool.

While beans are cooking, cut the baguette on the bias into 1-inch slices. Drizzle each piece with olive oil and a little salt. Place on a baking sheet and toast in the oven for 5 minutes. Remove and set aside to cool for 2 minutes.

Place a small skillet over medium heat, add 1 tablespoon olive oil, garlic, and rosemary, and sauté until garlic is fragrant, 1 to 2 minutes. Place mixture in a medium bowl and add cooked beans, remaining olive oil, lemon juice, and parsley (reserve a little) and toss. Smash the beans up a bit with a fork.

Spread some of the mash on top of each toast, drizzle with a little olive oil, salt, and pepper, and garnish with parsley.

Crispy Brussels Sprouts Chips

Serves 4 to 6

1 pound brussels sprouts, washed and dried
½ tablespoon extra-virgin olive oil

½ teaspoon kosher salt
Sea salt

Preheat the oven to 200°.

Remove bottom ends of the sprouts and discard. Cut each in half, peel, separate the leaves, and place them in a large mixing bowl. Drizzle with olive oil and kosher salt and toss lightly until fully coated.

Transfer sprout leaves to a large baking sheet and roast on the top rack until leaves are crispy and brown, but not burned, 15 to 20 minutes.

Transfer to a serving dish, sprinkle with sea salt, and serve.

Crispy Kale Chips

3 bunches black kale, stems removed and leaves torn
into pieces

2 tablespoons extra-virgin olive oil
Sea salt

Preheat the oven to 400°.

In a medium mixing bowl, toss torn kale with olive oil and salt. Spread evenly on a large baking sheet. Roast until crispy, about 15 minutes. Transfer to a serving bowl and serve.

Mains

Roasted Chicken

A good roasted chicken is the definition of coziness to me. I roast one almost every Sunday and watch as each member of my family casually sneaks by and picks off their favorite bits while it cools from the oven. For me, it's the crispy skin. The aroma fills my house and lingers most of the day; it's the gift that keeps on giving. On top of being amazing as an entrée fresh out of the oven, the leftovers can supply several more dishes. Shred leftover meat before you refrigerate it and it'll remain tender enough to use later in a salad, and store the bones in the fridge or freezer to make a chicken stock later.

If you don't have a cast-iron vertical pan, a roasting pan will work.

Serves 4

1 whole organic chicken (I prefer Mary's free-range)
¼ cup extra-virgin olive oil
3 tablespoons smoked paprika

2 teaspoons ground cumin
2 teaspoons garlic powder
Sea salt and freshly ground pepper

Preheat the oven to 400°.

Bring chicken to room temperature and pat dry.

Whisk together olive oil, paprika, cumin, garlic powder, salt, and pepper—it should look like a paste. Using a brush, coat the chicken with the spice paste. Hands work, too!

Place chicken in a cast-iron vertical roasting pan. Place it in the middle of the oven and roast until the internal temperature of the chicken reaches 160°, 35 to 40 minutes. Remove from the oven and let sit for 10 minutes, then slice and serve.

MELINA'S HACK

Put your favorite veggies or potatoes in the bottom of the pan, and all the chicken drippings will ooze onto your veggies.

Pork Chops

Pork chops are the first thing I recall my dad making for me when I was very young. It is so dear to me and carries such a sense of nostalgia that when I started cooking for my parents at age eight, I wanted to re-create it perfectly. It was the first thing I cooked for them—and the first dish that I eventually perfected, with help from my dad. He would serve it with fries, and I do the same today (but now they're oven-baked). I add some freshly sliced tomatoes and sautéed mushrooms for a quick and healthy meal that the entire family loves.

Serves 4 to 6

2 to 3 organic eggs
Sea salt and freshly ground pepper
1 cup Toasted Breadcrumbs (recipe on page 69)

¼ cup chopped flat-leaf Italian parsley
1 to 2 tablespoons extra-virgin olive oil
4 to 6 thin bone-in pork chops

In a small mixing bowl, whisk together eggs, salt, and pepper.

In a separate bowl, add Toasted Breadcrumbs and parsley and lightly toss together.

Heat a large skillet with olive oil over medium heat. Fully coat each pork chop on both sides with the egg mixture, then dip each side in the breadcrumbs mixture. Pan-fry until golden brown, about 3 minutes. Flip over and fry for another 2 to 3 minutes. Do not overcook.

Bone-in Ribeye Steak

Don't be skurred of cooking a steak. It really is the most simple thing to do. All you need is the right cast-iron skillet, a good cut of meat, some butter, and a lot of salt, then add a little patience and it will be perfect. Honestly, your friends will think you're a grill master. If you really want to impress, add some rosemary to your skillet in the last few minutes and fry that up with your steaks. The aromatics will take you right to heaven.

Serves 2

2 1½-pound bone-in ribeye steaks
Kosher salt

Canola oil
3 tablespoons butter

Generously salt steaks on both sides. Set aside to bring them to room temperature, about 30 minutes.

In a cast-iron skillet, heat some canola oil until sizzling but no longer (do not burn). Drop steaks into the skillet and cook on high heat until seared, 4 to 5 minutes. You want the bottom of each steak to be brown and crusted. Flip over and sear for another 4 to 5 minutes for medium rare. While they cook, place 1½ tablespoons butter atop each steak, spooning it back on to the steaks after it melts.

Transfer steaks to a cutting board to rest for 8 to 10 minutes. Remove the bone, slice across the grain, and serve.

I know I said "generously" salt the steaks—but what I should have said is "aggressively" salt the steaks.

Ginger Soy Salmon

This Asian-inspired salmon is soft-baked, tangy, and a little salty—you can't go wrong with that. Because it is packed with flavor and rich in texture, I would suggest pairing it with simple sides to avoid overwhelming your palate: rice or lentils with a steamed or sautéed veggie like broccolini are great choices.

Serves 4

1 tablespoon extra-virgin olive oil

3 tablespoons soy sauce

1 tablespoon mirin

1 teaspoon Dijon mustard

1 teaspoon whole-grain mustard

2 tablespoons rice vinegar

2 teaspoons finely minced (or microplaned) fresh ginger

1 tablespoon clover honey

1½ to 2 pounds deboned salmon

Preheat the oven to 350°.

Add olive oil, soy sauce, mirin, mustards, rice vinegar, ginger, and honey to a mixing bowl. Whisk thoroughly.

Pat salmon dry with paper towels. Place it skin side down on a medium baking sheet. Pour the ginger-soy glaze over the fish and gently massage it into the flesh on both sides.

Place baking sheet on the middle rack in the oven and roast until flaky with an internal temperature of 145°, 18 to 22 minutes. Remove from the oven and set aside to rest for 5 minutes. Once rested, transfer carefully to a serving platter.

Parchment-Baked Halibut

If you're anything like me, you sometimes find yourself with veggies deep in the fridge that you'd planned to use but never got to. This baked halibut is a perfect way to use them up. While I prefer this particular mix, don't shy away from adding in the odds and ends you have. No veggie left behind! Sealing them up to steam with the fish imparts a delicate flavor to everything. One and done.

Serves 4

4 sweet mini peppers, sliced
¼ cup thinly sliced fennel bulb
6 rainbow carrots, sliced lengthwise
1 tablespoon fresh thyme
2 sprigs rosemary

1 tablespoon extra-virgin olive oil
Kosher salt
4 6-ounce fresh halibut fillets
¼ cup dry white wine
Juice of 1 lemon

Preheat the oven to 375°.

In a mixing bowl, combine peppers, fennel, carrots, thyme, and 1 sprig of rosemary with olive oil and a pinch of salt.

Stack 2 large sheets of parchment paper, large enough to wrap all the fish and veggies in, on a baking sheet. Lay the halibut on top of the 2 layers of parchment. Pour white wine over the fish, salt each side of the fillets, and pour lemon juice over the fish. Top with vegetable-herb mixture.

Fold the paper over the fish and vegetables, from one side to the other and on either end, securing tightly. I use twine to tightly secure the package, so the steam doesn't escape. Tie the remaining rosemary sprig to the top for an extra touch. Bake for 28 to 30 minutes.

Transfer to a serving tray, still in the parchment, and untie the package at the table.

This is the perfect recipe for using up all the leftover vegetables you have in your fridge.

Mama's Chicken Soup

The remedy for everything. My mom used to make this chicken soup with an Armenian twist for me when I was a kid anytime I came down with something. It always perked me right up, and I could taste the love she put into it. Now I make it whenever someone gets sick in my house, as well as when they're healthy and it's chilly outside. This soup keeps in the refrigerator for about five days.

Serves 4 to 6

1 sprig fresh rosemary

1 sprig fresh oregano

1 bay leaf

1 sprig fresh thyme

1 herb sachet (or twine for tying)

1 whole organic chicken with skin on (I prefer Mary's free-range)

1 tablespoon kosher salt

1 white onion, cut into quarters

1 half lemon, plus lemon wedges for garnish

4 stalks celery, sliced

3 large carrots, sliced

½ cup white basmati rice, rinsed and soaked for 1 hour

1 cup chopped flat-leaf Italian parsley for garnish

Take the rosemary, oregano, bay leaf, and thyme and either place them inside the herb sachet or tie together with twine.

Place chicken in a large stockpot and add just enough water to cover the chicken (too much will make a weak broth). Add salt, onion, herbs, and half a lemon. Simmer over medium heat for 60 to 90 minutes, depending on the size of your chicken. If the broth begins to boil, reduce the heat. Scum/foam will begin to rise to the top; use a slotted spoon to remove and discard it.

When the chicken falls easily off the bone, it's ready. Remove the chicken from the broth and set it aside to cool.

Reduce heat to low and remove onion and herb sachet with a slotted spoon and discard. Add celery and carrots and simmer for 10 minutes. Drain rice and add to the broth. Simmer 5 to 6 more minutes.

While broth simmers, shred the chicken by using 2 forks to pull apart the meat into bite-size shreds. Add it to the broth and simmer another 5 minutes. The key is to simmer, not boil, the soup.

Before serving, remove the lemon, salt to taste, and serve by garnishing with parsley, a lemon wedge, and Simple, Perfect Bread (recipe on page 45).

MELINA'S HACK

Once the chicken is shredded, use half for the soup and save the rest for another day, to make a quick chicken salad sandwich or to add to any salad.

Spaghetti with Pancetta & Burrata

Hands down one of my very favorite pastas to serve, this spaghetti is well-balanced in acid and creaminess. Truly spaghetti at its best, this dish takes a classic to a new level.

SPAGHETTI

Serves 6 to 8

1 pound (or 17 ounces if it's packaged that way) dry spaghetti (I prefer Rustichella d'Abruzzo)

2 tablespoons kosher salt

2 tablespoons extra-virgin olive oil

Bring water to a boil in an 8-quart pot over a high flame. Add pasta and salt, and cook until al dente (approximately 6 minutes, depending on your pasta). Carefully drain the water from the pasta, reserving 1 cup of pasta water.

SAUCE

3 cups diced pancetta (medium dice)

1½ cups thinly sliced scallions

10 ounces double-concentrate tomato paste (I prefer Mutti)

1½ cups tomato purée (I prefer San Marzano)

1 cup reserved pasta water, divided

Al dente Spaghetti (recipe above)

Juice of 1 lemon

½ teaspoon ground chile flakes

1 cup grated Parmigiano-Reggiano cheese and/or Pecorino Romano

6 to 8 ounces burrata cheese, divided

Extra-virgin olive oil for garnish

Sea salt and freshly ground pepper

¼ cup Toasted Breadcrumbs (recipe on page 69)

Sauté pancetta in a large saucepan over medium heat, stirring occasionally, until it is almost crispy, about 5 minutes.

Reduce heat to low, add scallions, and sauté, stirring constantly, for 1 to 2 minutes. Add tomato paste, tomato purée, and ⅓ cup pasta water. Simmer on low heat for 10 to 15 minutes.

Add cooked Spaghetti and a dash of reserved pasta water, and toss until completely coated. Add lemon juice and chile flakes, and toss lightly. Remove from heat and add grated cheese.

Arrange pasta on plates. Top each with some of the burrata and add a drizzle of olive oil, a dash of sea salt, and a grind of pepper to each. Finish with Toasted Breadcrumbs and serve immediately.

MELINA'S HACK

My favorite cheese blend is a 50/50 ratio of parmesan and pecorino. If you can't get pecorino, using all parmesan will work just fine.

Bacon Macaroni & Cheese

My daughter thinks she hates cheese, but she's obsessed with this dish. I came up with it because I got tired of eating the same mac 'n cheese dish everywhere, and I kept experimenting to make it better. Sometimes I leave out the bacon, and if I'm making it for my family or a dinner party, I add blue cheese. With or without bacon or blue cheese, it's a gooey, sloppy, beautiful dish that is always a hit.

Serves 8

4 cups dry elbow pasta

Pinch sea salt

30 slices bacon, uncooked

1 medium white onion, chopped

2 teaspoons chopped fresh thyme

1 stick (8 tablespoons) unsalted butter

½ cup flour (I prefer King Arthur)

4 cups whole milk, divided

⅛ cup Worcestershire sauce

2 cups shredded parmesan

1 cup shredded sharp white cheddar

2 cups shredded gruyère, divided

¼ cup Toasted Breadcrumbs (recipe on page 69)

Preheat the oven to 350°.

Bring water to a boil. Add pasta and a pinch of salt to the water and cook for about 3 minutes, stirring occasionally. It'll be undercooked, but don't worry; it's going to get cooked more later. Drain the water from the pasta, reserving 1 cup of the water to use later. Set pasta aside.

Cut the raw bacon into 1-inch pieces (tip: using kitchen scissors will quicken this process). Sauté the bacon in a skillet over medium-high heat until crispy and browned, stirring occasionally, 12 to 15 minutes. Remove bacon from pan and set on a paper towel–lined plate. Discard (or set aside for later) almost all of the bacon fat, keeping about 1 teaspoon in the pan. You should end up with about 3 cups of cooked, chopped bacon.

Recipe continues on next page

Return the pan to medium-high heat. Add onion and thyme to the remaining bacon drippings and sauté, stirring occasionally, until the onion begins to brown, about 8 minutes. Remove pan from heat and set aside.

Next, you'll make the béchamel sauce. Make sure to have all your ingredients for it measured out before you start. Melt butter in a medium saucepan over low heat. When it's melted and starts to brown, slowly stir in flour. Then slowly add the milk, 1 cup at a time, whisking constantly.

Turn up the flame to medium heat and bring the mixture to a light simmer. Add Worcestershire and the onion-thyme mixture and whisk until sauce is thick, about 5 minutes. Remove from heat.

In a large mixing bowl, place pasta (if it's sticking together, add a little of the reserved pasta water), 2½ cups of the cooked bacon, parmesan, white cheddar, 1 cup of the gruyère, and the béchamel sauce. Thoroughly mix everything together with a wooden spoon until the pasta is coated in the sauce and cheese.

Pour the pasta mixture into a 13-by-10-inch oven-safe baking dish, making sure it's evenly distributed. Bake for 25 minutes. Remove from the oven and sprinkle with remaining gruyère and bacon as well as the Toasted Breadcrumbs. Return to the oven and bake for 5 more minutes. Remove and set aside for 5 to 8 minutes, so it sets up and isn't runny before serving.

MELINA'S HACK

I always keep some leftover pasta water in the fridge, so I can add a little of it to any pasta leftovers I'm reheating. Pasta water has magical powers to bring a dish back to life. When reheating plain cooked pasta, boil a bit of pasta water and flash-boil the pasta to revive it. To warm up a premade dish like mac 'n cheese, stir in a tablespoon or two to regain some of the moisture previously absorbed by the pasta. Reheat and enjoy!

Lamb Meatballs

Far more tender than beef, these lamb-and-pork meatballs practically melt in your mouth. Much lighter in texture than most meatballs and almost fluffy, they're stewed in the delicious acidity of spicy tomatoes. This sauce has a kick, so use just one chile to turn the heat down a notch.

TOMATO SAUCE

3 tablespoons extra-virgin olive oil

½ white onion, chopped

3 garlic cloves, minced

3 to 4 large carrots, peeled and minced

1½ cups minced celery

1 cup vegetable stock

1 28-ounce can peeled tomatoes (I prefer San Marzano)

1 28-ounce can puréed tomatoes (I prefer San Marzano)

1 5-ounce can double-concentrate tomato paste (I prefer Mutti)

½ teaspoon chile flakes

2 chile de árbol pods

Sea salt

Gremolata (recipe on next page) for garnish

In a large saucepan, add olive oil, onions, and garlic and sauté over medium heat, stirring occasionally, until onions are translucent. Add carrots and celery, stirring occasionally, until the vegetables begin to sweat, 5 to 7 minutes. Add vegetable stock and continue to stir occasionally until fully reduced, when no more liquid is evident.

Add peeled tomatoes, crushing them as you lower them into the pot. Add puréed tomatoes, tomato paste, chile flakes, chile de árbol pods, and a heavy pinch of salt. Bring to a simmer, add the Meatballs (recipe on next page), making sure that they are fully covered by the sauce. Simmer, stirring from time to time, for at least 30 to 35 minutes (the longer, the better!). Remove chile pods, taste, and add salt if needed. Serve and garnish with Gremolata (recipe on next page).

Recipe continues on next page

MEATBALLS

Makes 28 to 30 meatballs

½ cup whole milk

3 pieces white bread (crusts removed and cut into large cubes)

½ pound chopped pancetta

1 tablespoon anchovies

½ cup roughly chopped white onion

1 tablespoon minced garlic cloves (about 3 cloves)

½ bunch flat-leaf Italian parsley

10 whole mint leaves

1 tablespoon ground cumin

¼ tablespoon ground chile flakes

1¼ pounds ground lamb

1¼ pounds ground pork

1 tablespoon olive oil

Pour milk into a small bowl and add the white bread, allowing the bread to soak up the milk as you prep the meat for the Meatballs.

In a food processor, add pancetta, anchovies, onion, garlic, parsley, mint, cumin, and chile flakes. Begin to process together to create a paste-like consistency.

In a large mixing bowl, combine the lamb, pork, and pancetta mixture. Once fully combined, add the milk-soaked bread. Work the bread into the meat mixture until the ingredients are combined. Once incorporated, wet your hands and shape mixture into about 2-inch Meatballs. Place on a baking sheet or plate and set aside.

Heat olive oil in a pan over a medium flame. Sear Meatballs until browned, about 2 or 3 minutes per side.

Once all the Meatballs are seared, add them to the Tomato Sauce simmering on the stove (recipe on previous page).

GREMOLATA

2 tablespoons finely chopped flat-leaf Italian parsley

Zest of 1 lemon

¼ cup freshly grated parmesan cheese

¼ cup Toasted Breadcrumbs (recipe on page 69)

Combine all of the ingredients in a small bowl and serve as a garnish over the Meatballs.

MELINA'S HACKS

If you're entertaining, make the Meatballs a little smaller and serve them as an appetizer. And if you have leftovers, make some plain pasta and there you have it: an amazing pasta and meatball dish!

Sides

Burrata, Fennel, Hazelnut & Citrus Salad

While easily composed, this salad leans on the side of elegance and is more appropriate for a plated sit-down dinner. The ingredients aren't complicated, and in their purest and rawest form, they speak boldly for themselves. The colors and shapes build a gorgeous plate, making this an impressive start to any meal.

Serves 6

½ cup hazelnuts

6 mandarin oranges, peeled

5 blood oranges, peeled

4 Cara Cara oranges, peeled

1 medium fennel bulb, with fronds

6 4-ounce balls burrata cheese

Extra-virgin olive oil

Sea salt and freshly ground pepper

Preheat the oven to 300°.

Roast hazelnuts on a medium baking sheet until golden brown, 7 to 10 minutes, then set aside to cool. Once cooled, chop them roughly.

Slice the oranges into ¼-inch-thick rounds. Arrange 3 to 4 slices of each on the plates in a random pattern, letting them overlap a bit here and there.

Trim off fennel tops and set them aside. Carefully slice the fennel bulb as thinly as you can, then scatter the slices (6 to 8 per plate) and hazelnuts (4 teaspoons per plate) atop the citrus. Set a ball of burrata in the center of each plate.

Drizzle with olive oil and garnish with fennel fronds (7 to 8 per plate), a little sea salt, and pepper.

Butter Lettuce Salad with Poached Eggs

Because their season is so short, English peas should be eaten only at their peak of freshness. If they're not in season, another kind of crisp veggie will work just fine. The poached egg is optional, of course, but it does add a beautiful creaminess and pop of color. When plating this salad for a dinner party, stack the lettuce like pancakes for gorgeous height. Freshness is the key to this salad, so serve it right after you make it.

Serves 4

2 large heads butter lettuce

1 medium avocado, thinly sliced

½ small watermelon radish, thinly sliced (use a mandoline if you have one)

½ pound English peas out of the pod (keep a few intact in the pods for garnish)

¼ cup English pea tendrils (if available)

4 Poached Eggs (recipe follows), optional

Sea salt and freshly ground pepper

3 teaspoons Toasted Breadcrumbs (recipe on page 69)

Grainy Mustard Vinaigrette (recipe on page 68)

Remove the cores of each lettuce head, then carefully peel open the lettuce, making sure to keep the leaves intact. Rinse the leaves in ice-cold water to remove any debris, then set aside and pat dry.

This salad can be plated on one large platter or on 4 individual plates. Whichever you choose, layer lettuce leaves in a mound in the middle of the plate. While building height, layer avocado and radish slices, peas, and tendrils randomly around the salad.

Place Poached Eggs (if using) on top of the salad, and add salt and pepper to taste.

Garnish with a couple of peas in the pods. Sprinkle evenly with Toasted Breadcrumbs and drizzle Grainy Mustard Vinaigrette over the salad and eggs. Serve immediately with extra dressing on the side.

POACHED EGGS

2 tablespoons white vinegar

4 eggs, room temperature

Bring 3 cups water and vinegar to a boil. Reduce to medium heat and carefully crack the eggs into the water. Cook for 2½ minutes. Carefully remove each poached egg with a slotted spoon.

Roasted Heirloom Carrots with Sumac Crème Fraîche

This dish is such a winner. I love the Middle Eastern flavor profile, and the acid of the pomegranate pairs so well with the earthy sweetness of the carrots and the tanginess of the crème fraîche. It's rich in color and has such a *wow* factor, which makes it great for entertaining.

Serves 4

2 bunches heirloom carrots

Extra-virgin olive oil

Sea salt and freshly ground pepper

½ cup Sumac Crème Fraîche (recipe follows)

2 tablespoons pomegranate seeds

¼ teaspoon sumac

½ teaspoon finely chopped flat-leaf Italian parsley

Preheat the oven to 400°.

Scrub the carrots and cut off the tops, leaving 1 inch of each top intact. Place carrots in a large mixing bowl, drizzle with some olive oil, sprinkle with salt and pepper, and mix until the carrots are completely coated.

Transfer carrots to a baking sheet and roast until slightly blistered with some char, 15 to 18 minutes, shaking the pan back and forth after 7 minutes to promote even cooking.

Plate the carrots in a pyramid-style stack and pour a ribbon of Sumac Crème Fraîche over the top. Garnish with pomegranate seeds, sumac, parsley, and sea salt.

SUMAC CRÈME FRAÎCHE

This doesn't just go with carrots—it's delicious with almost anything. Sumac is a classic Persian spice, and it reminds me of where I came from.

Makes 1 cup

1 cup crème fraîche

1 teaspoon ground coriander

½ teaspoon ground cumin

½ teaspoon sumac

½ teaspoon chili powder

½ teaspoon sweet paprika

Sea salt and freshly ground pepper

Add all ingredients into a medium mixing bowl and whisk until evenly mixed. Taste and add more salt and/or pepper if needed. Transfer to a small bowl, cover, and store in the refrigerator until needed, for up to 1 week. Remove from the refrigerator 30 minutes before using.

Roasted Cauliflower
with Pine Nut Purée

Vegetarians and meat eaters alike love this dish. If you can't find purple or yellow cauliflower, white cauliflower will look just as beautiful. While this dish has several components and might seem intimidating, each part can be made ahead of time and will hold, refrigerated, for a couple of days beforehand, so you just have to cook the cauliflower before serving. And because it tastes great at room temperature, it can sit for a while. Additionally, you don't *have* to pull out all the stops if you don't have time—just one or two components will be delicious. If you're cooking for vegans, leave out the Pine Nut Purée.

Serves 4

2 heads purple or yellow cauliflower
4 tablespoons extra-virgin olive oil, divided, plus
more for garnish
Juice of 2 lemons, divided

Sea salt and freshly ground pepper
1 cup Pine Nut Purée (recipe on next page)
Salsa Verde (recipe on page 147)
1 ¼ cups Pine Nut Relish (recipe on next page)

Preheat the oven to 350°.

Trim the outer leaves and stems of the cauliflower heads and cut them horizontally into 1-inch pieces.

Arrange the cauliflower evenly on a small baking sheet. Drizzle with 2 tablespoons olive oil, juice of ½ lemon, and a pinch of salt and pepper. Flip and repeat with remaining olive oil, juice of ½ lemon, salt, and pepper.

Roast on the top oven rack for 10 minutes. Turn cauliflower over and roast an additional 15 minutes, so both sides are browned, increasing heat to broil for the last 2 minutes. Set aside to cool.

To arrange the composed dish, smother a serving platter with the Pine Nut Purée, covering the plate. Top with Salsa Verde, then layer with cauliflower pieces. Top with Pine Nut Relish, a heavy drizzle of olive oil, a heavy pinch of salt, and the juice of 1 lemon. This should be served at room temperature.

Pine Nut Purée

Makes 1 cup

¾ **cup Roasted Pine Nuts (recipe follows)**

¾ **cup whole milk**

Pinch kosher salt

In a small saucepan, add Roasted Pine Nuts, milk, and salt. Stir and bring to a light simmer. Once it begins to simmer, reduce heat and begin to stir constantly, bringing it to a light boil. Remove from heat and allow to sit for 10 minutes. Pulse this mixture in the food processer for about 2 minutes to achieve a thick consistency, then remove and set aside.

Pine Nut Relish

Makes 1 ¼ cups

½ **cup currants, rehydrated in 1 cup warm water**

6 **tablespoons Roasted Pine Nuts (recipe follows)**

2 **tablespoons finely chopped shallots**

2 **tablespoons chopped flat-leaf Italian parsley**

1 **tablespoon Champagne vinegar**

2 **tablespoons extra-virgin olive oil**

Toss all ingredients together in a medium mixing bowl and set aside.

ROASTED PINE NUTS

Preheat the oven to 325°. Place 1 cup, plus 2 tablespoons, pine nuts on a small baking sheet and roast until lightly browned, about 12 minutes. Set aside to cool.

Salsa Verde

Makes ½ cup

1 medium garlic clove, peeled

2 canned anchovies

2 cups chopped flat-leaf Italian parsley

2 cups fresh mint leaves

1 teaspoon fresh oregano

Juice of 1 medium lemon

½ teaspoon kosher salt

3 tablespoons extra-virgin olive oil, divided

Place garlic, anchovies, parsley, mint, oregano, lemon juice, and salt in a food processor. Begin to pulse together and slowly add olive oil 1 tablespoon at a time. Continue to process until fully puréed.

Persian Panzanella

1 small red onion, thinly sliced

4 Persian cucumbers, sliced

1 pound heirloom cherry tomatoes

2 tablespoons extra-virgin olive oil

Juice of 1 lemon

2 teaspoons rice vinegar

1 teaspoon sumac

Sea salt and freshly ground pepper

¼ cup crumbled feta cheese

1 cup Hand-Torn Croutons (recipe on page 69)

In a medium bowl, toss together onions, cucumbers, and tomatoes.

In a small bowl, whisk together olive oil, lemon juice, rice vinegar, sumac, and salt and pepper. Pour over salad and toss to coat with dressing. Add feta and Hand-Torn Croutons and toss just to combine. Taste and add more salt and pepper if needed.

Roasted Vegetables

This is a rustic dish: Throw all your veggies in one pot, toss in some rosemary and garlic, pair it with your favorite proteins, and you have a perfect meal with no fuss! If you don't have these vegetables on hand, use what you have. Just remember that some will roast faster than others, so put in the heartier ones first, then add the more delicate ones at the halfway point.

Serves 4 to 6

1 bunch baby rainbow carrots, washed and sliced lengthwise

½ pound baby brussels sprouts, sliced in half

½ head cauliflower, washed and sliced

4 to 5 whole cipollini onions

1 bulb garlic, sliced in half and roughly chopped

½ pound broccoli florets

Extra-virgin olive oil

Sea salt

4 sprigs fresh rosemary, finely chopped

Preheat the oven to 375°.

In a mixing bowl, toss all the vegetables with olive oil, salt, and rosemary. Make sure they all get coated with oil.

Arrange the vegetables evenly on a baking sheet. Place on the middle oven rack and roast for 20 minutes. Using a wooden spoon, stir the vegetables and return to the oven, roasting for another 10 or 15 minutes. Increase the heat to broil and cook 5 more minutes to get a nice crisp.

Fingerling Potatoes

So easy and so delicious, these potatoes go well with almost everything. They're a perfect side dish.

Serves 4

1 pound fingerling potatoes

2 tablespoons butter

3 garlic cloves, smashed

3 sprigs fresh rosemary

Kosher salt and freshly ground pepper

Cover the fingerlings with water and a pinch of salt, bring to boil over high heat, then reduce to a simmer and cook for about 10 minutes. They're ready when a fork can easily pierce through them. Drain and slice potatoes in half lengthwise.

In a skillet or saucepan, melt butter and add garlic cloves and rosemary. Add potatoes and sauté, stirring occasionally, until browned. Season to taste with salt and pepper and serve.

Desserts

Okay, call me crazy, but I am so much more of a savory person than a sweet person. I don't know if it's genetics, but my kids are exactly the same way (maybe this explains my love for lemons). Don't get me wrong, though—I will never turn down a great chocolate soufflé, but give me some salted caramel pudding and you'll find me curled up on the couch, in my sweats, watching reruns of *NCIS* or *Real Housewives*…with my yellow Lab helping me lick the bowl clean.

Jagger's First Cake

Baking wasn't my favorite thing to do—until I had my little girl, Jagger. Her first birthday cake wasn't the perfect shape or the prettiest cake, but seeing her face as she took her first bite made it so worth the effort. Ever since then, I wanted to make cakes for every birthday party and cupcakes for every school bake sale. Though I don't always have time to as a working mom, this recipe makes it simple and fast enough for when I don't have a ton of time to put into an elaborate production. And it suits my preference for a cake that's not overly sweet—I like my sweetness to be in the frosting.

When I had my son, River, five years later, I made him the same cake for his first birthday. By then I'd had more years of practice, and I have to say it looked much better than my first attempt. That said, don't focus on what it ends up looking like. Between the kind gesture and the taste, the person you're baking for will love it! You can always pretty it up or hide a funny section with fresh flowers. You don't even need a stand mixer to make it.

The most important thing is to make sure ALL of your ingredients are at room temperature before you start. If you buy your ingredients the day you're making the cake, don't even refrigerate them when you return from the store.

This is a good base recipe that you can adapt in many ways. It can be made as a sheet cake or in two or three layers—it's entirely up to you. (Just remember that baking times will vary.) For cupcakes, scoop the batter into muffin tins. You can also experiment with variations by adding lemon or orange zest, cocoa powder, or confetti sprinkles; some food coloring and a bit of cocoa powder will make it a red velvet cake. Just don't get too carried away, so you don't change the balance of the ingredients and ruin your batter.

Makes 1 8-inch 3-layer cake

2¼ cups flour (I prefer King Arthur)

2 cups sugar

1 teaspoon salt

2 teaspoons baking powder

12 tablespoons butter

6 large egg whites, room temperature

1 cup whole milk, room temperature

2 teaspoons vanilla extract

Preheat the oven to 350°. Butter 3 8-inch cake pans.

In a small mixing bowl, sift together flour, sugar, salt, and baking powder. Add butter, 2 tablespoons at a time, and knead together with the flour mixture to form small crumbles. Continue until all the butter is added and set aside.

In a large mixing bowl, slowly whisk together egg whites, milk, and vanilla extract. Slowly incorporate the dry ingredients until batter is smooth.

Pour batter evenly into each pan and bake until cooked through and a toothpick comes out clean, 20 to 25 minutes. Remove from oven and set aside to cool while you make the frosting.

Jagger at the table.

Frosting

This is a very simple frosting. The most important note is to make sure your butter and cream cheese are at room temperature, or the butter chunks will NEVER smooth out of your cream cheese. Any leftover frosting will keep in the fridge and can be used to frost cupcakes later.

16 ounces cream cheese, room temperature
1 cup (2 sticks) unsalted butter, room temperature
2 teaspoons fresh lemon juice
1 tablespoon lemon zest

1 teaspoon vanilla extract
4½ cups confectioners' sugar
Edible flowers for garnish

In a large mixing bowl, whisk together cream cheese and butter until smooth. Add lemon juice, lemon zest, and vanilla and whisk together. Slowly stir in confectioners' sugar and continue whisking until frosting is smooth and without clumps. Place in the refrigerator for about 30 minutes.

FROSTING THE CAKE

When you're ready to assemble the cake, carefully remove one of the layers from its pan and set it on a 15-by-15-inch piece of parchment paper. Dollop a generous spoonful of frosting on top. Using a palette knife (a long, flat spatula) or a rubber spatula, evenly spread frosting to the edges. Set another cake layer on top and frost the top the same way, then repeat with the final layer. Spread remaining frosting down the sides of the cake. Turn the spatula vertically and smooth the frosting across the sides of the cake while turning the parchment paper so the cake rotates, adding additional frosting where needed until you have an even, smooth coating.

Decorate with fresh flowers.

Pomegranate & Balsamic Sundae

I know what you might be thinking—ice cream and vinegar?! Don't let me lose your trust just yet! The amazing Nancy Silverton of Mozza created an olive oil gelato years ago that blew me away. She inspired me to try something a little more adventurous with my own ice cream at home. While I won't force you to make your own ice cream from scratch, I will strongly suggest that you try this incredible drizzle. When the balsamic reduces, its sugars begin to caramelize and the vinegar flavor dissolves into a tangy, tart syrup that pairs perfectly with pomegranate seeds, although you can also use whatever favorite fruit is in season. The flavor is sophisticated enough to serve on plain vanilla ice cream.

Serves 4

8 scoops vanilla ice cream (I prefer Häagen-Dazs)

4 tablespoons Balsamic Reduction (recipe follows)

¾ cup roasted thinly sliced almonds

½ cup fresh pomegranate seeds

Edible flowers (optional)

Put 2 scoops of ice cream into 4 bowls. Lightly drizzle with Balsamic Reduction. Sprinkle with almonds and pomegranate seeds, garnish with a few edible flowers (if using), and serve immediately.

BALSAMIC REDUCTION

2 cups balsamic vinegar

¾ cup brown sugar

In a saucepan, bring vinegar to a simmer over medium heat. Add brown sugar and cook, stirring continuously, until the sugar has dissolved. Reduce heat to low and simmer until the glaze reduces, 15 to 20 minutes. Let cool before using.

MELINA'S HACK

When making a balsamic reduction, the glaze is ready when it sticks to the back of a spoon.

Salted Caramel Pudding

I'm not sure what is more delicious: John Legend, my newborn's butt, or this salted caramel pudding. You be the judge.

Serves 8

1 cup sugar

⅓ cup water

4½ cups milk, room temperature, divided

1 vanilla bean, split lengthwise

6 egg yolks, room temperature

5 tablespoons cornstarch

1 tablespoon sea salt

2 tablespoons butter, room temperature

Whipped Cream (recipe follows)

Prep each of your ingredients before you begin, as you will need to keep an eye on each step of the cooking process to prevent burning or boiling over.

Place sugar and water in a medium saucepot over medium heat. Cook until amber in color, being careful not to burn the sugar water. Pour in 4 cups milk a little bit at a time, swirling the pot between each addition. The milk will steam and splutter, so be careful not to add too much at once. Scrape out the inside of the vanilla bean and add the scrapings to the mixture. Cook mixture until it scalds and remove from heat.

Whisk together egg yolks, remaining ½ cup milk, cornstarch, and salt in a large glass or Pyrex bowl, blending well to ensure there are no lumps. Slowly pour in the scalded caramel milk a little at a time, whisking well between each addition. This will "temper" your egg mixture, preventing it from curdling. Once it's all combined, pour mixture back into the pot and return to medium heat.

Cook, scraping with a rubber spatula against the bottom of the pot every couple of minutes to prevent burning. When it begins to thicken and bubble lightly around the edges, remove from heat immediately, as overcooking the egg yolks (beyond 180 degrees) will curdle them and give your pudding a clumpy and watery texture. Stir well and pour through a fine-mesh strainer. Whisk in butter while hot.

Divide equally into 8 5-ounce ramekins. Top each with about 1 tablespoon Whipped Cream and chill at least 90 minutes. Before serving, add a pinch of salt to each pudding.

WHIPPED CREAM

Makes 1½ to 2 cups

1 cup heavy whipping cream

2 teaspoons vanilla extract

2 tablespoons sugar

In a medium metal mixing bowl, whip cream with a whisk or hand mixer until stiff peaks are just about to form, about 10 minutes. Add vanilla and sugar and continue to mix just until peaks form. Don't whisk any more than that, because the cream can become lumpy.

Olive & Thyme

Beck's Dutch Apple Pie

I would be lying if I said this wasn't inspired by my dearest friend, Rebecca, and her mom, Mary Jo. Any holiday that I was able to spend in Kentucky in their beautiful home brought the amazing aroma of this pie. It isn't a complicated recipe, and remember, you can always buy a premade crust if you need to. It's worth it, though, to make it at home. You can do it!! You will never go back to store-bought!

Makes 1 pie

TOPPING

⅔ cup all-purpose flour (I prefer King Arthur)   ⅓ cup butter

⅓ cup light brown sugar

Combine flour and sugar in a medium bowl. Using a pastry cutter, cut in the butter until the mixture has the consistency of coarse cornmeal. Refrigerate for 30 minutes while you make the filling.

FILLING & PIE

2 pounds (5 to 6) Granny Smith apples, cored and   ½ cup sugar
   peeled   Pinch sea salt

1 tablespoon fresh lemon juice   1 teaspoon ground cinnamon

2 tablespoons all-purpose flour   1 unbaked pie crust

Preheat the oven to 400°.

Using a mandoline, thinly slice apples into a large bowl and sprinkle with lemon juice. In a medium bowl, stir together flour, sugar, salt, and cinnamon. Add to apple mixture and toss lightly. Spoon filling into pie crust, spreading evenly. Cover with topping and bake for 1 hour. Check at 40 to 45 minutes, and if the topping is too brown, cover loosely with foil and finish baking.

NO BETTER NO BUTTER PIE CRUST

1¼ cups sifted all-purpose flour, plus more for   ½ teaspoon sea salt
   dusting   ⅓ cup vegetable oil

Sift flour with salt into a medium mixing bowl. Add oil and mix with a fork. Add 2 tablespoons cold water and continue to mix until smooth. Don't be afraid to use your hands! Form dough into a ball.

Sprinkle some flour onto a cold surface and, using a floured rolling pin, roll out dough to about ⅛ inch thick and about 12 to 13 inches around. Roll dough onto your rolling pin and lay it over a 10-inch pie pan. Gently form dough into the pan. Cut off any excess dough and pinch the edges. Fill with your pie ingredients. You can make this ahead of time; just wrap tightly and freeze it.

Blackberry Crumble

Baking is often scientific and not a skill easily acquired without practice, so when I first started having dinner parties, I had to come up with a good, simple dessert that I could make. I remembered a crumble that blew me away at this amazing LA restaurant called Cynthia's, and I kept experimenting with crumbles until I re-created the flavor that I remembered. Crumbles became my go-to dessert for dinner parties. They are simple to make, and everyone loves them.

You can make crumbles with all kinds of fruit; I just really love the flavor of blackberries and how they hold their texture when they're cooked. Berries and stone fruit are staples in my house, and they're so easy to put together for a quick dessert.

Serves 8

8 5-ounce oven-safe ceramic bowls
6 cups fresh blackberries
2¼ cups brown sugar, divided
3 teaspoons cornstarch

½ cup all-purpose flour (I prefer King Arthur)
6 teaspoons softened unsalted butter
8 scoops vanilla ice cream (I prefer Häagen-Dazs)

Preheat the oven to 400°.

In a large mixing bowl, add blackberries, ¾ cup brown sugar, and cornstarch. Lightly toss until blackberries are fully coated but no longer, so you don't smush the berries. Set aside.

In a separate mixing bowl, place flour, butter, and remaining 1½ cups brown sugar. Use your hands to lightly mix the ingredients together. The butter will create little balls when mixed with the sugar and brown sugar.

Set the ceramic bowls onto a baking sheet. Equally distribute the berries into each bowl, and then evenly sprinkle the crumble mixture on top of each.

Place on the center rack in the oven and bake until the crumble starts to turn golden brown and the berries start to bubble, 40 to 45 minutes. Set aside to cool for 5 to 10 minutes. Add a scoop of ice cream to each and serve.

Entertaining

Let's be real, people, you're just throwing a party. It is no different than your sweet sixteen, except now you're the adult and you have to throw things together and cook, but the overarching principles are still the same. You have to think ahead, don't get ambitious and kid yourself with the menu, and, most importantly, have fun. People are there to be with you and enjoy themselves. Sometimes it's easy to get caught up in the details—and don't get me wrong, the details are important—but if you have a checklist, a good playlist, and some chilled wine, the rest will all fall into place.

My Philosophy Behind Entertaining

Entertaining is about providing the right environment and setting for people to connect and enjoy themselves. It doesn't matter whether it's an intimate dinner for two, cocktails with your neighbors, a baby shower with your girlfriends, or an all-out kids' party for your firstborn. The reality of it is this: Whether it's the planning, the cooking, or the hosting (all the "fluff"), the goal is to create an opportunity for people to detach from their everyday stress for a few hours. To remember what's really important in life: meaningful connections with one another.

The philosophy couldn't be more simple, but getting there can take some practice. My early experiences cooking for my family gave me a glimpse of this concept, but years of trial and error have taken me from running around like a crazy woman to hanging out with my guests, enjoying the moments, and, best of all, watching everyone else have fun. What's the point of entertaining if you're stressed out? You should have just stayed at work, where you get paid.

Here are a few of the basics:

THE MENU

I'm all for experimenting, but definitely not when you are entertaining. Design a menu that you're comfortable cooking, so you know you can execute it well and you're familiar with the timing. Your tried-and-true dishes are your best bet to achieve a result that you already know is delicious—and that won't stress you out! Save the experiments for another time when there's less on the line.

Choose a menu that will allow you to do as much prep in advance as possible, so you won't be stuck in the kitchen when you should be relaxing and enjoying your guests. What sounds better—having your guests arrive when you're in your sweatpants, hair still up, and dishes piled in the sink while you're sweating over the stove—or enjoying a cocktail while listening to some old-school hip-hop while getting your prep work out of the way, cleaning as you go, and allowing yourself some time to relax before your guests arrive? I've been in both situations—and trust me, the first scenario ain't pretty.

Meeting new people is hard enough, so cook something that is welcoming instead of intimidating. I wouldn't cook quail or rabbit for a dinner party—unless I was hosting a dinner for my chef or foodie friends. When I entertain, I make roasted chicken, steak, or pasta—food you can't go wrong with. There's nothing more awkward than a table full of people hesitant to eat because they don't know what's on their plate. Don't forget to include an option for everyone; I always make sure there's at least one delicious vegetarian or vegan dish and have an enticing mocktail.

CLEAN AS YOU GO

If I can teach you anything, it is clean as you go—that's one of the most important lessons I have learned over the years. I remember those early parties in my little apartment. Friends would arrive to see all my drawers and cabinets open and my sink piled with dirty dishes. It was a disaster. At the end of the night, when everyone was gone, I'd be stuck with two hours of cleanup. Trust me when I tell you: No one wants to wake up the day after a party and clean up. Make your new motto Clean as You Go. It's simple: Use a pan, wash a pan, then wipe down your counters, fold your dish towels, and start to prep your next item. This takes a little practice, but once you perfect it, you will never go back. This will not only change your life, but it will make you a better cook. Soon you'll be the Marie Kondo of your kitchen—the lack of cleanup at the end of the night will bring you so much joy.

SETTING THE TABLE

I'm a big believer in using your natural environment for table décor: branches, flowers, herbs, get creative! The Thanksgiving after I'd just had my first baby, the last thing I was thinking about was cooking a holiday dinner. But of course, the mom guilt kicked in the day before and I looked for a butcher who'd have a last-minute standing rib roast for me to cook. I got through the cooking with some effort but had no time or energy to plan decorations. Twenty minutes before our guests were set to arrive, my sweet husband, Christian, walked down the street to collect leaves, pinecones, and anything he could find that made sense. His last-minute effort made our table look incredible. We added some fresh rosemary from the garden and pumpkins that were on our front porch, and it was such a personal creation that was so special to all of us. This was a perfect lesson that I wasn't expecting to learn: Even during the times that I've planned the most, and have had the most resources, I've found that it wasn't really necessary...and it isn't for you either! If you allow yourself to relax, breathe, and not make a big deal about it, no one else will. Let yourself get creative, and release some control.

If you're serving your food family-style—which is my favorite way to entertain—use a few tricks to make the spread look more abundant. When I have more than eight people, I like to split each of my dishes into two platters at each end of the table. This makes it easier for guests to reach each dish without having to wait ages for it to be passed, plus it makes the table seem more generous.

I kick it old-skool when it comes to place settings—I like to have a salad fork and a dinner fork. I think it lends a nice touch, but it doesn't mean it has to feel stuffy and it definitely doesn't mean you have to assign seating. In fact, I prefer a more organic flow when it comes to seating. Don't feel pressured to do place settings; just be comfortable. At the end of the day, remember that it's not about how many forks or wine glasses you have; it's about being in the moment. Just take it easy.

PAIRING PEOPLE

The guests in your home are *so* much more important than what's on the menu or how stylish your décor is. Hosting family and friends is an opportunity to spend quality time with loved ones, as well as to foster deeper connections between those who may not be so close yet. That being said, don't force it! If you know your mom and mother-in-law aren't the best of friends, let's not seat them next to each other. Everyone will thank you!

When hosting friends, I try to be thoughtful in connecting people. When a new friend visits my house, I introduce them to somebody who's familiar with my home, who knows that I have an open-door policy—which means they know they can reach into my fridge and pour themselves another glass of wine, or they know where we keep the good snacks hidden in the cabinets. The hope is that the next time our "new" friend comes to visit, they'll feel as though they can do the same thing. At times this can feel like a fault, but most of the time it is the greatest gift you can get.

This is another reason why you don't want to get stuck in the kitchen. You want to make sure everyone is getting along and enjoying themselves. Trust me, no one will remember your food or flowers if your crazy neighbor is hitting on your best friend's husband.

COCKTAIL PARTIES

A cocktail party, happy hour, girls' night…it's all about hanging out and having fun. When your friends walk in the door, give them a drink and make sure there's something to eat. A grazing board or a couple of platters filled with cheese and charcuterie or crudités and hummus are essential. Boards and platters provide a great place for people to gather, have a glass of wine, chat, and decompress from the day. If you are a coaster person, have some linen cocktail napkins set out—don't make your friends guess whether they can set their drink down or not. Check out vintage stores to find linen cocktail napkins and unique glassware. It's a great way to add elegance without breaking the bank.

When it works, I like to have fun with elegant place settings.

DINNER PARTIES

Dinner parties typically start with a cocktail hour, which lets people relax and get to know one another. An hour is about the right time, but at my house it's ninety minutes, since no one is ever on time in LA! Make sure you're there to welcome your guests during the first part of your cocktail hour, but feel free to slip away for a bit to finish up in the kitchen before serving.

If it's a small dinner party and it's plated, everyone should sit down at the same time. Your guests will not sit down until you do, so make sure you're not stuck searing that last piece of steak when it's time for dinner. I try to avoid seating arrangements, unless it's something more formal, like a holiday dinner or a business meeting, where I want to connect certain people. I don't think adults want to be told where to sit. Once everyone is seated, it's important to say something: Give a toast, welcome your guests, thank everybody! Say a few words about why you gathered this group—there's a reason you asked them to join you. No pressure: A simple Cheers! will do if that's your style.

If someone is late to a small dinner party, do them a favor and wait ten to fifteen minutes before serving dinner, and as the host, make sure you greet them. They feel bad enough that they are late.

If someone is kind enough to bring you flowers, don't just discard them onto the counter; place them in water. They took the time to stop and get you flowers, so show them the same respect and take the time to take care of their gift. The thoughtfulness will be appreciated.

When dinner is said and done, dessert doesn't need to be seated or complicated. After an hour and a half of sitting, people usually want to get up and move around. If you have the room, transition to the living room or patio. Offer an easy dessert or even some sliced fruit and a digestif.

SPECIAL EVENTS

Whether it's a baby shower, an engagement party, or a kid's birthday, a celebratory event needs a plan. It's a good idea to have a light schedule and a checklist to make sure you're not scrambling to bring out the birthday cake just as half your guests are ready to leave. I like to cut out opening presents at these events, to keep the flow of the party going. We've all seen a onesie, a kid's toy, and a toaster get unwrapped—gifts can be opened later! Also, feel free to decorate beyond the typical pink and blue for a baby or white for a bride-to-be. It's not the 1960s anymore, so don't feel limited!

I think a brunch set up family-style works best for these types of events. Plan a couple of games or an activity if you're into it, like making a wish book with Polaroids of your guests with a sweet note. Send your guest of honor home with something that will remind them of the special day—it adds an extra touch.

LARGER PARTIES

I've never been a fan of the word *buffet*—it makes me think of chafing dishes, cruise ships, and all-you-can-eat Vegas restaurants. Despite that, large parties actually flow better when you have family-style stations. I decorate these areas with a more organic feel, adding natural elements like flowers, eucalyptus, or lavender. Instead of chafing dishes, I keep hot dishes in my Le Creuset pots with lids, both because they hold heat well and because they don't have that stuffy look that chafing dishes have.

Get creative with flowers for a dessert table.

Usually I'll have some food to pass around. If hiring servers isn't in your budget, set up a cheese and charcuterie board in one area and a crudité platter with a couple of types of hummus in another. That will spread out the areas where people gather.

My rule of thumb is to cook four main dishes and provide platters as well. They can all be prep-ahead dishes: perhaps a baked salmon for a protein, with seasonal roasted vegetables, a room-temperature rice salad, and a generous green salad. Four dishes, plus a few boards or platters (which are arranged, not cooked), provide plenty of variety, which makes guests happy. If you are making a big dish, like a lasagna or a roast, put out half or a quarter of it at a time. That also allows you to keep the rest of it warm. Dessert can also be handled on platters; good options are cookies or bars made in advance. Don't be afraid to have desserts already set out on a different table, and remember, there is no bad time for dessert!

Keep your menu in line with your event. For instance, if it's a backyard barbecue, have traditional barbecue offerings. If it's a kid's birthday party, make sure there's something for everybody, including picky kids, kids with allergies, and adults. For a family party, have a kid-friendly choice, like a simple pasta or chicken dish. I often see parties where the food is either totally kid-focused or totally adult-focused. It's so easy to cover both!

A big party is a lot of work, but it's also freeing, because you can let go of the notion that everyone has to eat at the same time. Try not to interrupt conversations—let it flow, let people eat when and what they want, and let them feel they can keep going back for more over and over again! Just make sure to refresh the food so it continues to look bountiful, and keep the table clean—no one wants to eat off a picked-over, dirty table.

MUSIC

Music is a crucial part of entertaining. I truly believe that your playlist is just as important as your food. It sets the stage, and when it's done right, it puts everyone in a good mood. Think of it as your first course, and just like your menu, make sure it's tailored to your guests. If I'm having my parents over, I'm definitely not blasting Metallica.

Whatever music you settle on, keep an ear on the volume. It can be a little louder during cocktail hour, but it should always be background music, so it provides a subtle mood but doesn't overtake the conversation. As much as I love music, I love a good conversation more.

THE DETAILS

The details really matter, and not just when it comes to the food. In the restaurant world, we call this curb-to-curb hospitality: You want people to feel welcome from the moment they park until the moment they leave.

As I've said before, keep your kitchen as tidy as possible. The bathroom is also super important. Clean it thoroughly in advance, light a candle, put in a fresh roll of toilet paper, have hand towels out, and keep an extra one in a drawer so you can switch it out if you need to. When you visit the bathroom, wipe down the counter and refold the hand towels.

Have a place for guests to put coats and purses when they arrive, and when it comes time for them to leave, consider offering a small takeaway gift as a token of their time with you. I love sending my guests home with some preserved lemons (see page 64), a seasoning I particularly like, or some fresh herbs from my garden. Add a few words in a special note, something to remind your guests of the amazing evening they had. I always email my guests the next day to thank them and to share the playlist from the party.

The most important thing about entertaining is to be present and in the moment. Set yourself up so you can be part of the party instead of just working the party. Always remember that the people you invited have come to be with you. Although the details and the food are important, the memories you make will have the biggest impact. Have fun, enjoy your friends, and eat!

CHECKLIST

Here is an easy checklist to follow when you are throwing a party:

- Make a Plan
  - Create a timeline
  - Have a plan B (for example: What if it rains and you'd planned to host everyone outside?)
- Food & Beverage
  - Prep your dishes either the night before or the morning of the event
  - Pull the cheese out of your fridge early enough for it to come to room temperature
  - Chill wine and other beverages
  - Make sure you have ice to chill your beverages as well as to serve in drinks
  - Wipe your glasses down—you don't want fingerprints or water marks on them
- House Prep
  - Sweep outside
  - Vacuum inside
  - Dim the lights
  - Make sure you have fresh water in your vases
  - Make sure it smells fresh
  - Fix drapes and curtains so they are in place and even
  - Set the table and make sure the place settings are straight (I always suggest setting your table early in the day, so later you can just focus on the cooking)
  - Straighten your dining chairs
  - Have a place for your guests to put their coats and purses
- Fresh Flowers
  - Entrance
  - Tables
  - Guest bathroom
  - Coffee tables
  - Main entertainment area
- Candles
  - Trim your wicks
  - Wipe off any black soot from the candles
  - Light ten minutes before guests arrive
- Bathroom
  - Wipe down the countertops
  - Put out fresh hand towels
  - Put out new soap
  - Light a candle
  - Add a new roll of toilet paper
  - Empty the trash
- Seating
  - If you have pets, make sure your couch and seating areas are hair free!
  - Fluff your pillows
  - Wipe down coffee tables and set out candles
- Turn on your music and set the volume correctly
- Be dressed early and give yourself at least thirty minutes to pour yourself a cocktail and have some down time before your guests arrive

I like to make a children's party a family party, so everyone can celebrate together, even the alpacas! Throw down a bunch of pillows and blankets in different areas to add texture and create a great place for adults and kids to hang out. It exudes a welcoming and casual feel.

Boards & Platters

Fruit Platter

The best part about making your own fruit platter? You don't have to use unripe melon. We've all suffered through the hard melon found in those expensive grocery-store fruit platters. When you make your own, you can use the ripest, most colorful fruit while spending less.

The main rule: Always use what's in season. I especially love citrus season, with the gorgeous hues found in blood oranges, mandarins, tangelos, and kumquats. Berry season brings another range of rich colors. You don't have to play it safe with the fruits everyone knows—experiment with dragon fruit, star fruit, persimmon, papaya, or pomegranate. They'll turn a fruit platter into a conversation piece, and you just might introduce a guest to a new favorite food.

You can make something so simple look so elegant with just a bit of thoughtful planning. Choose fruits that have a pop of color, and avoid putting fruits with the same dimensions or heights near one another. Consider getting creative with remnants from prepped veggies. Save carrot tops and place them beneath sliced fruit, tuck berries into red cabbage leaves, or arrange pea tendrils at the edge of the platter. Fresh herbs like mint add fragrance and greenery, a good contrast to the warm, bright colors of fruit. Finally, when prepping your fruit, keep the stems and tops on—they may not always be edible, but they're easy to eat around and add a natural touch to the platter.

Fruit is delicate, so it's best when prepped and arranged on the day you'll be serving it, and preferably not more than a couple of hours ahead. Cutting up fruit the night before can make it dry or mushy, because it starts to break down in your refrigerator once it's cut.

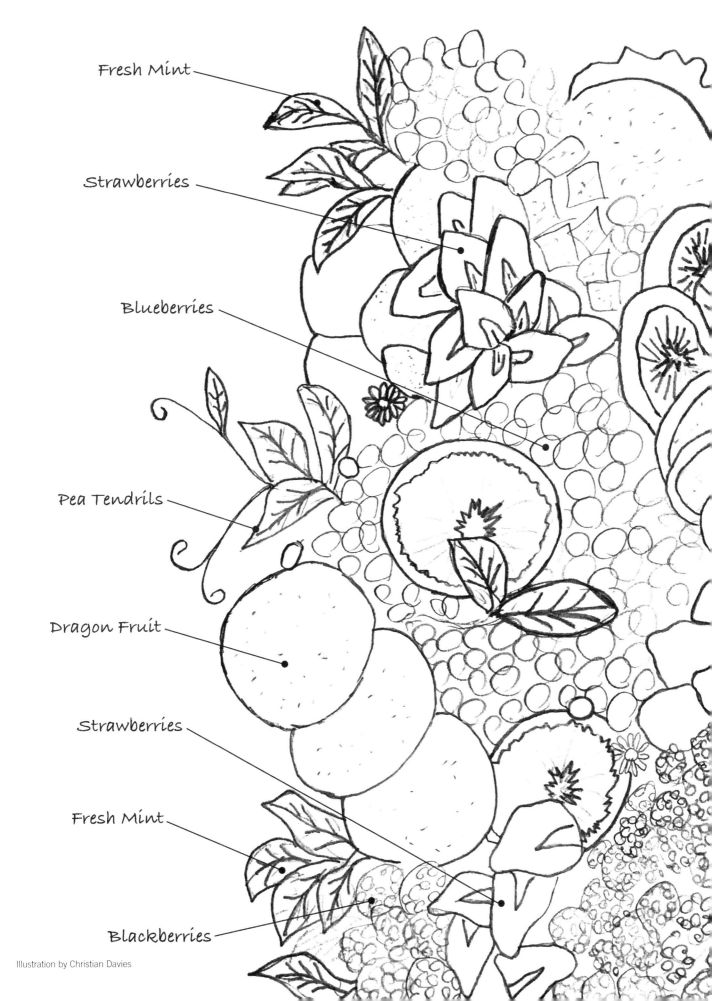

Fresh Mint

Strawberries

Blueberries

Pea Tendrils

Dragon Fruit

Strawberries

Fresh Mint

Blackberries

Illustration by Christian Davies

Lox & Bagel Board

The concept here is simple: Put everything you could think to put on a bagel on a platter. Everything on a lox and bagel platter can be prepped and set ahead of time, *except* for the lox and toasted bagels; you'll want to do those last.

Everyone loves a bagel platter, even if they don't like lox! Different flavors of cream cheese—jalapeño, chive, sun-dried tomato—can add variety to your platter, as will colorful ingredients like cucumbers, capers, jalapeños, avocado, and red onions. Set out your lox and toast your bagels a few minutes before your guests arrive, and call it a day!

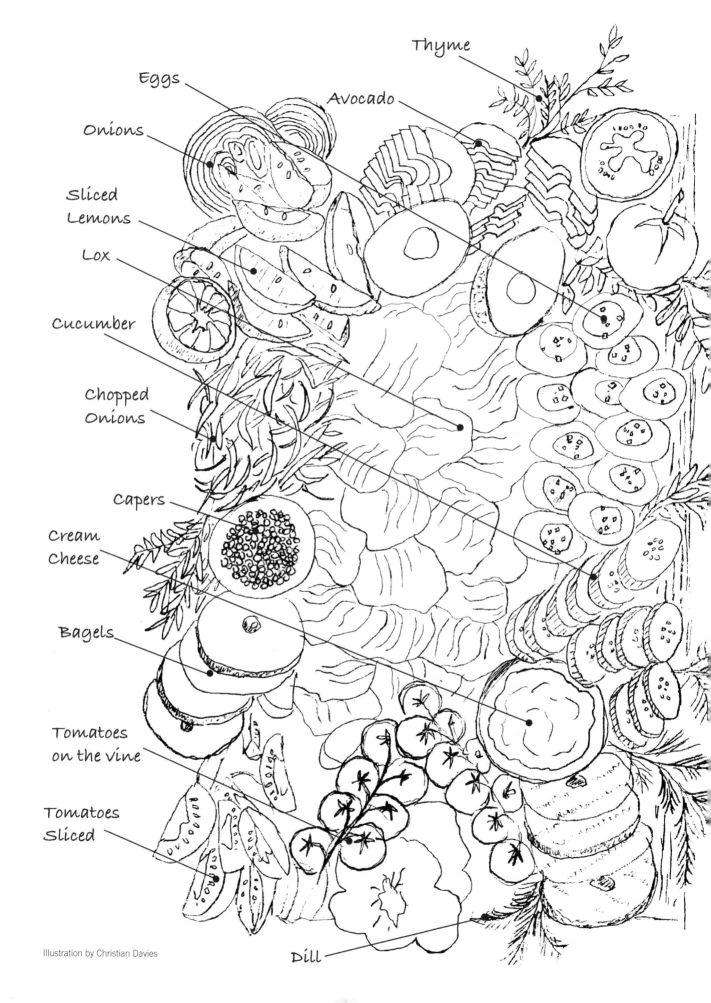

Thyme

Eggs

Avocado

Onions

Sliced
Lemons

Lox

Cucumber

Chopped
Onions

Capers

Cream
Cheese

Bagels

Tomatoes
on the vine

Tomatoes
Sliced

Dill

Illustration by Christian Davies

Cheese & Charcuterie Board

I'm literally obsessed with cheese, charcuterie, and wine. That's the first reason I fell in love with France. The second reason was the architecture, the third was the fresh baguettes, and the fourth was the men (that was before I was married, of course).

Traveling through Europe taught me so much about cheese. Fortunately, in recent years the US has made great strides in cheese production, and it's now much easier to find gourmet cheeses at many local grocery stores. With the number of quality cheeses available, no one should feel intimidated by a cheese plate!

Whether making a cheese and charcuterie board that's six feet long or a plate for two people, the basic rules still apply. It's all about the balance: of flavors, of textures, of colors, of shapes. Below are the components of any good board.

CHEESE As a general rule, you'll want to have three to four kinds of cheeses, depending on the number of people you're feeding: a hard cheese, like a manchego or a pecorino; a semisoft or triple crème cheese, like Brillat-Savarin; and a blue cheese, like Saint Agur. If you're not too into blue cheese, try something more palatable, like Shropshire.

Here are some of my favorite cheeses:

Bay Blue (Point Reyes Farmstead Cheese Co.)	Midnight Moon (Cypress Grove)
Brillat-Savarin	Mt. Tam (Cowgirl Creamery)
Époisses (not for the faint of heart!)	Saint Agur
Hook's 10-Year Cheddar	Shropshire Blue
Humboldt Fog (Cypress Grove)	Tomme Fleur Verte

CHARCUTERIE If you have the option, get your charcuterie freshly sliced from a butcher. Ask the butcher to slice it so thin that it's almost translucent—you want the fat to melt in your mouth as soon as it touches your tongue. I love to include prosciutto di Parma, a fennel salami, and a bresaola on my platters for a variety of textures and flavors.

NUTS Marcona almonds are essential—they're an easy-to-find nut that everyone likes. I also tend to use pistachios, but you can include whichever ones you prefer. With their soft texture and fat content, cashews and walnuts are also great options.

CRACKERS I like to have two varieties: typically, toasted baguette slices, which go with everything, and a nut-and-seed cracker to pair well with dried fruits and jams.

Continues on next page

SWEET Fig paste is a cheese-board staple, as its sweetness offsets the pungent flavors of some of the more adventurous cheeses. Cherry and quince pastes are lovely and tart alternatives, and honeycomb will add another layer of sweetness and texture. As for fruit, at least one dried stone fruit (apricots, cherries, or dates) is a must, as well as any fresh fruits in season; I love figs, and berries are always welcome in the mix.

TANGY A good board calls for an acidic component, such as cornichons or olives. On a big board, you can get away with both. My favorite olives are the firm, bright green Castelvetranos from Sicily, which are creamy, buttery, and mild.

HERBS Fresh sprigs of herbs add fragrance and color; rosemary is my favorite. Consider cherry tomatoes on the vine, and cut a few little flowers from the garden for beauty—they don't have to be edible, and they'll take your presentation to the next level.

MELINA'S HACK

If you don't have a lot to spend on cheese and charcuterie, you can still make a big, gorgeous platter—just sub in some farmers' market produce. Generous mounds of accompaniments will more than make up for a modest quantity of fine cheeses. Try adding half an artichoke, avocado halves, an array of rainbow carrots, cucumbers, radishes, and/or sliced strawberries, all of which will add volume, color, and flavor.

Oh, how I love French cheeses, like the Provençal goat cheese tomette à l'huile and the Saint-Nectaire and Saint Agur blue.

TOMETTE A L'HU
4€
4.40 PIÈCE.

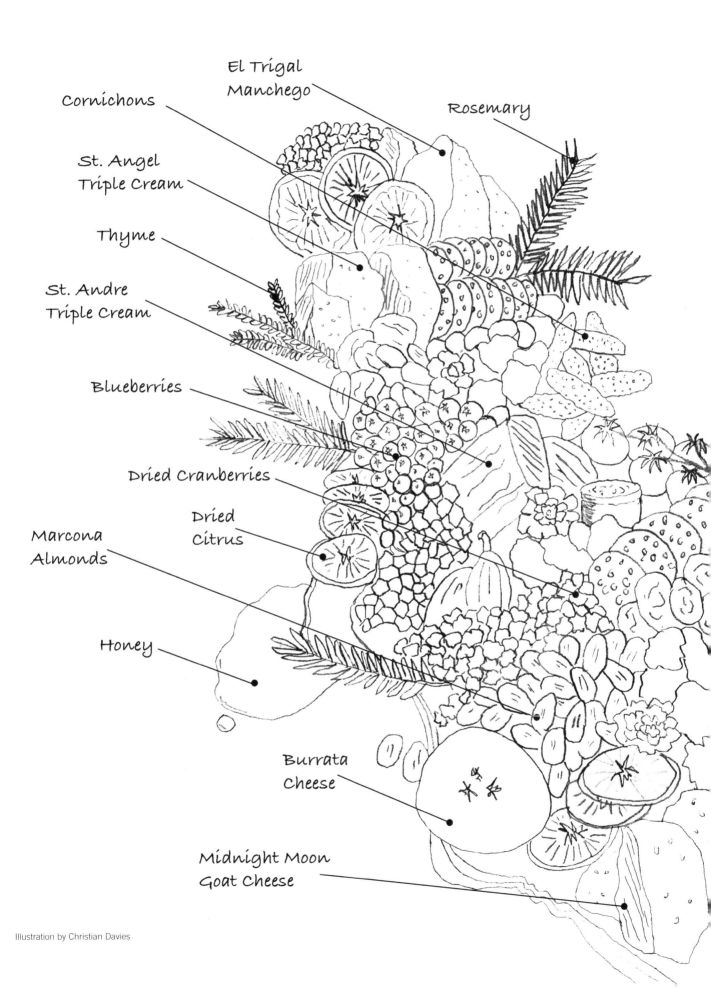

Cornichons

El Trigal
Manchego

Rosemary

St. Angel
Triple Cream

Thyme

St. Andre
Triple Cream

Blueberries

Dried Cranberries

Dried
Citrus

Marcona
Almonds

Honey

Burrata
Cheese

Midnight Moon
Goat Cheese

Illustration by Christian Davies

Roasted Rosemary Cashews

Makes 1 cup

1 cup raw cashews
1 teaspoon sea salt
½ teaspoon sugar

½ teaspoon cayenne
1 tablespoon finely chopped rosemary
1 tablespoon melted butter

Preheat the oven to 350°.

Place cashews on a baking sheet and roast until lightly browned, 10 to 11 minutes.

Combine salt, sugar, cayenne, rosemary, and butter in a medium mixing bowl and stir to combine. Add cashews and toss to combine. The mixture will keep for up to 1 week.

Crudités Board

One of my happiest memories of my travels in Europe was sitting by the sea one summer and being served a basket of raw vegetables with an anchovy vinaigrette. It was one of the most simple yet elegant creations I'd ever seen, filled with produce of the season in its most natural element, vibrant and bright in color. That became one of my favorite things to eat outdoors. Whether they were filled with heirloom carrots, radishes, endive, parsley, or fresh tomatoes on the vine, they were always crisp, clean, and satisfying. I brought that inspiration home. Unfortunately, not everyone loves anchovies (I'm not sure why!), but hummus is a great option—it's vegan, it's kid friendly, and it can be made in so many variations. You'll find two of them on the following pages, and also try the Beet Hummus on page 53.

Olive & Thyme's Famous Hummus

I can honestly say that this is the best hummus in town: smooth, just the right amount of tahini, and richly delicious. Use it on your sandwiches if you're avoiding mayo!

Makes 2½ cups

3 cups drained chickpeas

4 garlic cloves

¼ cup tahini (I prefer Mid East Sesame)

½ cup fresh lemon juice

5 tablespoons extra-virgin olive oil

1 teaspoon kosher salt

½ teaspoon freshly ground pepper

Paprika for garnish

In a food processor, add chickpeas, garlic, tahini, and lemon juice and process together for 5 to 6 minutes. This mixture should become like a paste.

Slowly pulse in the olive oil until the mixture has a smooth, creamy texture. Add salt and pepper, and continue to process the mixture slowly until combined. Transfer to a serving bowl and dust with paprika. Serve with warmed naan bread or fresh crudités.

Carrot Hummus

Makes 2 cups

5 large carrots, peeled and sliced in half lengthwise

2 garlic cloves

Extra-virgin olive oil

Pinch of sea salt

1 tablespoon fresh lemon juice

½ teaspoon ground cumin

1 tablespoon fresh orange juice

1 cup Olive & Thyme's Famous Hummus (recipe
   on facing page)

Carrot shavings for garnish

Preheat the oven to 400°.

Place carrots and garlic on a roasting pan, drizzle with olive oil, and sprinkle with salt. Place in the oven on the top rack and roast until carrots are fork-tender, 35 to 40 minutes. Set aside to cool.

When cool, cut into 2-inch pieces and place in a food processor. Add 2 tablespoons water, lemon juice, cumin, orange juice, and Olive & Thyme's Famous Hummus. Process together until fully blended. Garnish with carrot shavings and serve with warmed naan bread or fresh crudités.

The hummus will keep in the refrigerator for up to 4 days.

The Perfect Grazing Table

There are times when I just want to have some friends over, put my feet up, enjoy a glass of wine, connect with my loved ones, and not worry about what I'm going to cook. My perfect solution to keep me out of the kitchen is to build a grazing table. The way to do that is to find a large area in your home where you can gather everyone around a communal space, and put together a variety of fresh fruits, raw vegetables, herbs, nuts, crackers, charcuterie, and cheeses. A grazing table turns food into art, becomes the focal point, and immediately transforms your party into a community event, all with very little work. All you have to do is follow a few basic guidelines, which you'll find on the following pages.

HOW TO BUILD A GRAZING TABLE

- Build a frame with herbs and dried citrus
  - It makes people reach into the middle of your board to get food, encouraging interaction, and a frame will help prevent your vision from being immediately destroyed
- Color blocking
  - Keep like colors together
- Use seasonal vegetables and fruits
  - Summer: peaches, other stone fruit, berries, cherries, citrus, grapes, snap peas, cherry tomatoes, cucumbers
  - Fall: persimmons, kumquats, crab apples, cauliflower, squash, endive
  - Winter: pomegranates, cranberries, pears, turnips, brussels sprouts
  - Spring: apricots, mangoes, broccoli, rhubarb, radicchio
- Use your vegetables to build height
- Use the tops on all your produce as garnish
- Use whole fruits and vegetables
  - Cut some of them in half and in quarters to give different dimensions to the board (for example: turnips, carrots, avocados, heirloom tomatoes, artichokes, cucumbers)
- Use edible flowers and regular flowers as garnish
- Use dried fruits and nuts
- Have at least three or four types of cheeses, and be knowledgeable about them so you can discuss with your guests
- Have three types of crackers
- It's always nice to have some honeycomb
- Use small matching bowls to separate items that have juice—like olives and cornichons—and use vegetables to cover the sides of the bowls, so it flows
- Make sure your cheese knives are all facing the same direction
- Don't be afraid to introduce people to new foods they might not know—like black radish, dragon fruit, and star fruit.
  - Have a paring knife close by so you can cut a piece for a guest if they're interested in trying it
- Adapt your grazing table to your guests' dietary preferences—it can be vegan or vegetarian
- Don't be scared to repeat the same story throughout the board

Cocktails

Bloody Mary

A Bloody Mary feels like a starter meal. My favorite is one that's really spicy and horseradishy, so that's what I've created with this recipe. I love to make a Bloody Mary bar when I entertain. While I prefer mine to be salty and spicy, it's fun to offer scotch as a smoky substitute for vodka, as well as a variety of hot sauces.

A common problem with Bloody Marys is that they get watered down by the time you're halfway through. On top of that, with the tomato juice, horseradish, and garnishes, they can be so filling. For those reasons, I serve them in smaller glasses with one large ice cube. This will keep the ice from melting too quickly and your drink from getting too watery.

Makes 1 drink

1 lime, cut in quarters

Black Cyprus sea salt

1 large ice cube (about 2 by 2 inches)

Regular ice

½ cup Fresh Tomato Juice (recipe follows; store-bought is also fine)

1 ounce fresh lemon juice

1½ teaspoons Worcestershire sauce

3 dashes Tabasco sauce

¼ teaspoon celery salt

2 teaspoons ground horseradish

1½ ounces vodka

Pinch sea salt and freshly ground pepper

1 celery stalk

3 pimento olives (optional)

2 to 3 pepperoncini (optional)

Rim a cocktail glass with a lime wedge and dip in Cyprus sea salt. Add 1 large, square ice cube. If you can't get a large ice cube, use a few smaller ones.

In a cocktail shaker, add ice, Fresh Tomato Juice, lemon juice, Worcestershire, Tabasco, celery salt, horseradish, vodka, and salt and pepper. Shake until combined and pour into cocktail glass. Garnish with a celery stalk and, if you'd like, olives and pepperoncini.

FRESH TOMATO JUICE

Take 3 to 4 heirloom tomatoes, blend in a food processor, and strain through a fine-mesh strainer.

Peach Bellinis

An homage to Harry's Bar founder Giuseppe Cipriani, this cocktail takes me back to the first time I visited Venice, Italy, and had my first Bellini. It was one of the most perfectly balanced drinks I've ever had. Tart and bubbly prosecco with delicately sweet white peaches—what more is there to say? Though you may not be on a Venice canal while sipping this drink, it's about as close as you can get.

Makes 6 to 8 drinks

5 peaches (preferably white), cut into quarters
3 tablespoons simple syrup

1 bottle prosecco, chilled

In a blender, add peaches and simple syrup and purée until completely smooth. Place in the freezer for 15 to 20 minutes to chill.

In a pitcher, combine 4 parts prosecco and 1 part peach purée. Serve immediately, so the Bellini stays chilled.

Mint Elderflower Vodka Lemonade

This screams summertime to me. I love a lemonade that's tart; my kids, on the other hand, do not. Whether I make lemonade to their preference or mine, vodka is always a welcome guest in my glass. Who says women don't compromise?

Makes 2 cocktails

2 tablespoons fresh mint, plus more
1½ ounces elderflower liqueur
3 ounces vodka (I prefer Tito's)

½ cup Lemonade (recipe follows)
Ice
Lemon slices for garnish

Place mint and elderflower liqueur in a shaker. Using a muddler or the end of a wooden spoon, gently muddle the mint just until it releases more aroma. Add vodka, Lemonade, and ice and shake together. Strain drinks into coupe glasses and garnish with mint leaves and lemon slices.

LEMONADE

Makes 10 cups

4¼ cups filtered water, divided
1½ cups granulated sugar

4 cups fresh lemon juice
Lemon slices and mint leaves for garnish

To create a simple syrup, in a saucepan combine ¼ cup water and sugar, and place over medium heat. Bring to a boil and dissolve the sugar, constantly stirring to ensure that the syrup remains clear. Remove from the heat and set aside to cool.

In a pitcher, combine simple syrup, remaining 4 cups water, and lemon juice. Stir until ingredients are fully incorporated. Serve over ice and garnish with lemon slices and mint if you'd like.

Watermelon Margaritas

Speaking of summertime, watermelon season means the tastiest margarita you've ever had. Sweet watermelon with a Tajín salt rim—*ridiculous!* Plus, watermelon is ultra-hydrating and contains Vitamins A and C, so you're giving your body a healthy dose with every drink. Or at least that's what we tell ourselves.

Makes 2 drinks

Juice of 1 lime

8 slices jalapeño, divided (4 slices muddled, 4 slices for garnish)

8 ounces fresh watermelon juice

4 ounces silver tequila (I prefer Casa Dragones)

Ice

Sea salt

Tajín

In a shaker, combine a little of the lime juice and 4 slices jalapeño. Using a muddler or the end of a wooden spoon, gently muddle the jalapeño. Add remaining lime juice, watermelon juice, tequila, and ice. Shake together.

Rim 2 cocktail glasses with lime, sea salt, and Tajín. Add ice and pour in margarita mix. Garnish with 2 slices of jalapeño in each glass and serve.

Aguas Frescas

These are a hit at the restaurant and at all my summertime parties—they're a lovely nonalcoholic beverage option, and kids love them.

Makes 10 to 12 drinks

8 cups of your favorite fruit, peeled and seeded

3 cups water

½ cup sugar

Fresh fruit for garnish

Combine fruit, water, and sugar in a Vitamix. (If you don't have one, make in 2 batches in a blender.) Blend until smooth, then pass through a fine-mesh strainer to remove the small bits. Pour into a pitcher and serve in a glass over ice, garnished with a slice of fruit.

Cotton Candy Champagne

The greatest thing about sparkling wine is that it doesn't have to cost you $500 to taste good. There are so many different variations and ways you can serve it, whether it's at a Sunday brunch, dinner with friends, or a kids' party (because let's be real—what adult doesn't need Champagne at a kids' party?). There is nothing better than a fresh mimosa during a brunch, that perfect Bellini on a hot summer day, or a crisp, dry glass of French Champagne when the sun is setting. One of my favorite tricks at a party is to throw in some cotton candy—it's delicious and interactive, the perfect way to kill two birds with one stone.

MELINA'S HACK

Got some prosecco or Champagne left over? If you don't have a stopper, just put the handle of a metal spoon into the neck of the bottle. The bubbles will last longer—it really works!

My Essentials

A well-stocked pantry leads to amazing meals. I've often found myself making the best meals by rummaging through what I have on hand. It's what leads me to experiment the most. In fact, that's one of the things I most love about cooking: There aren't many rules. The more comfortable you get with flavors and the ingredients of the season, the more confident you'll become in experimenting, and eventually you won't even need recipes.

Below are my key essentials; yours may vary based on your tastes. If you keep your pantry supplied, you'll always be able to whip up something amazing.

CANNED, DRIED & BOTTLED FOODS

Anchovies

Beans, dried (all varieties)

Capers

Chile paste

Cornichons

Flour, all-purpose (I prefer King Arthur)

Fresno chiles

Fruit, dried (apricots, cherries, dates)

Garbanzo beans (fresh)

Harissa paste (I prefer DEA)

Honey (I prefer clover)

Mayonnaise (Best Foods is the best)

Mirin

Mustard, Dijon, and grainy (I prefer Maille)

Olive oil, extra-virgin (an "everyday" one for cooking and a higher-quality one for salads, garnishing, and seasoning)

Olives, picholine

Soy sauce

Sriracha hot sauce

Stocks, chicken and vegetable (preferably make your own and freeze; if not, have packaged stocks handy)

Sugar, granulated, brown, and confectioners'

Tahini

Tomato paste, double-concentrated (I prefer Mutti)

Tomatoes, peeled and crushed (I prefer San Marzano)

Tuna, yellowfin in olive oil if possible (I prefer Genova)

Vinegar, red wine, rice wine, and balsamic (both an everyday grocery-store version and a higher-quality aged version)

SPICES

Aleppo red pepper

Cayenne pepper

Chile flakes

Chiles de árbol

Chili powder

Coriander (whole and ground)

Cumin (ground and seeds)

Fennel seeds

Madras curry powder

Mustard (dried)

Paprika

Peppercorns, black (in a grinder)

Salts, kosher, sea, garlic, and onion (I prefer Maldon sea salt)

Sumac

Tajín seasoning powder

Turmeric

Urfa

Za'atar

GRAINS

Farro

Pad thai rice noodles

Pasta (dried), especially penne and spaghetti (I prefer Rustichella d'Abruzzo)

Rice (basmati, brown, and arborio for risotto)

NUTS & SEEDS

Cashews (roasted)

Marcona almonds

Pine nuts

MY FAVORITE PRODUCE TO HAVE ON HAND

You don't need to have all this in stock! What you actually have on hand will, of course, depend on the season. Allow the season to tell you what to cook. Don't plan the menu first—let the farmers' market or the local produce aisle plan it for you.

Avocados

Beets

Bell peppers (I prefer yellow and orange)

Blueberries

Brussels sprouts

Carrots (heirloom if possible)

Cauliflower

Celery

Cherry tomatoes (heirloom if possible

Citrus (when in season)

Cucumbers (Persian)

Fennel

Garlic

Jalapeños

Lemons & limes

Mushrooms

Onions (white and red)

Parsley (flat-leaf Italian)

Potatoes (fingerlings)

Raspberries

Squash (acorn, butternut, spaghetti)

Strawberries

Sweet potatoes

Tomatoes (roma and/or beefsteak)

DAIRY & DAIRY ALTERNATIVES

Almond milk

Blue cheese (Saint Agur is my favorite)

Burrata

Butter (unsalted)

Cream (Straus Family Creamery's is my favorite)

Crème fraîche

Eggs (organic free-range)

Feta cheese (Bulgarian is my favorite)

Goat cheese

Milk (Straus Family Creamery's is my favorite)

Mozzarella

Parmigiano-Reggiano and/or pecorino cheeses

Soy milk

Triple crème cheese

Yogurt (European-style plain; I like Straus Family Creamery's)

Yogurt (Greek)

FRESH HERBS

Again, let the season determine which of these you keep on hand.

Basil
Bay leaves (fresh)
Chervil
Chives
Cilantro
Dill
Lavender
Mint
Oregano
Rosemary
Sage
Shallots
Tarragon
Thyme
Verbena

AND FINALLY...

Always make sure your pantry is stocked with your favorite bottle(s) of wine!

Index

Acknowledgments

When I was approached to write a cookbook, it was a dream come true—little did I know just how much work would go into it! Without all of these people, my dream would have never become a reality.

Christian, thank you for being my partner in everything. You are an incredible father, husband, and the most patient person I have ever met. You truly are my other half.

Jagger, my sweetest, kindest, most gentle girl. You are the light of my life and have taught me how to take a breath and realize what is really important in life. You have my heart.

River, my big-eyed, always-smiling baby boy. Life is so much fun with you in it. You are my little monster who makes me wish I could freeze time. I love you more than words can express.

Dad, this is all because of you. Thank you for believing in me and encouraging me to follow my dreams, no matter what the outcome. I am your biggest fan, and you will always be my number one. I am who I am because of you.

Mom, thank you for showing me what a true entrepreneur is. You've taught me what sacrifice and hard work mean.

Famor, the most loving grandma. My children are so lucky to have the most caring and gentle famor.

Fafa, we feel your presence in our hearts and are forever grateful for you.

Jeff, I don't know how I got so lucky to have someone like you trust in me. You are my guardian angel.

Keila, for your never-ending support, for allowing me to pee in front of you, have babies in front of you, and see me in my darkest times. You are literally my right hand–this book could not have happened without all of your hard work.

Edgar, I am so proud of you. Seeing you grow from a dishwasher to a chef reminds me of why I do what I do. You will always be a part of my family.

Kayra, clearly writing isn't my forte, and without you, this book would be filled with run-on sentences. You've been a part of my family for six years, and your devotion to me has been undeniable. I will forever be grateful.

Matty, you have been dedicated to my family and Olive & Thyme since day one. Your drive, passion, and eagerness continue to amaze me; I am blessed to

have you in my life. You really are the jack of all trades.

My O&T family, you are my second home. Thank you for your passion, hard work, and dedication to what we do. It takes a village, and each and every one of you is a part of that. You make me so proud.

Lindsey, my ride or die. Every time I've called, whether for help, in tears, or just needed some Taco Bell—you were there. You define friendship.

Eileen, the greatest manager. This is all your fault—and I could not be more grateful. Thank you for seeing something in me and believing in me.

Colleen, for your patience and understanding of my neuroses and my need for perfection. Thank you for trusting in me.

Ann, you shoot food beautifully. You sprinkled your magic fairy dust wherever it was needed. You are an angel, and it has been a pleasure to work with you.

Amy, thank you for your hard work and for seeing our vision the way that we see it. We could not have imagined a more beautiful cookbook.

Nancy, you are an inspiration, a role model, and my muse. You do what you do with such elegance and grace. I am forever amazed at your skill.

Jet, I have so much respect for what you do. You have been such a big supporter, and I am honored to have someone of your caliber recognize my passion.

Matt, you always take great care of me. Thank you for teaching me how to make my favorite pasta.

Reeves, thank you for your support over the years. You have always believed in me and always pushed me to be better in everything I do.

Melissa, I'll see you in the morning with a big hug.

Della, you welcomed me and my children into the Spago kitchen with open arms. You have the purest heart, and your talent supersedes all others.

Eric, stop stealing my cows.

Kevin, I will forever be grateful for all the guidance and support; because of you, I always take a moment thyme.

Keith, thank you for keeping me out of jail.

Vinny, you are a master of your craft, and I will forever be obsessed with your wife.

Ozzi, you took me under your wing when

all I wanted was a small sandwich shop. If it wasn't for you, I wouldn't be where I am today.

Jim, you saved my ass. You remind me why I should have been a lawyer. THANK YOU!

Ashley, you were thrown into this project without much notice, and due to your wildly incredible talent, have become a major part of it. Thank you for making me look good even when I don't always feel good.

Xochitl, thank you for loving my children and treating them like your own. They are so lucky to have a big sis like you.

Johnny & Carmen, without you both my life wouldn't run. You love and take care of my children, keep my life in order, and make my house a home. That, and Carmen's black beans are the best in the world.

Francesca, you will never forget how to tie the most perfect bow. Thanks for rushing me to the hospital when Jagger was born. I love you.

Armen, you show me the light and the simplicity of life. You are always my ear with zero judgement, and that is the most priceless gift you can give.

Kate, you always have my back. Thank you for all of the words of encouragement and for reminding me that it's okay to ask.

Bonjour Fête, no one does balloons like you guys do. You always help bring our parties to life.

Little Horse on the Prairie, words cannot express the love I have for you, Hunter, and the animals that you care for. The fact that you run such an awesome business by yourself and are always smiling amazes me. Fable and Whisper can come over anytime.

Lisa, the beautiful cakes your team at Cake Monkey Bakery made for our entertaining chapter were stunning as always. Thank you for always seeing my vision.

Those who believed in me in the beginning: **Rebecca**, **Dubin**, **Bob**, **Dave**, and **Kennedy**.

To all of my loyal guests: You've walked through our doors for the past nine years and treated us like your family—and you are definitely mine. I appreciate every one of you, and not a day goes by that I'm not grateful.

About the Author

Melina Davies is a self-taught cook who left a career in the movie industry in 2011 to open a tiny café called Olive & Thyme in Toluca Lake, California, later moving to a much larger location just up the street and most recently opening a second restaurant. The daughter of Armenian immigrants and a graduate of the University of Southern California, Davies lives in Studio City, California, with her husband and their two young children.

Photographer Ann Elliott Cutting's work has appeared in such books as *The Portable Feast* and *The Urban Forager* and such publications as *Time, The Washington Post,* and *Los Angeles.* She is associate professor of photography at ArtCenter College of Design. Also providing photographs for the book was Ashley Barrett, whose work has appeared in such magazines as *Glamour, Lucky,* and *ELLE.*

Published by Prospect Park Books
2359 Lincoln Avenue
Altadena, California 91001
www.prospectparkbooks.com

Distributed by Consortium Books Sales & Distribution
www.cbsd.com

Library of Congress Cataloging in Publication Data is on file with the Library of Congress. The following is for reference only:
Davies, Melina
Olive & Thyme: Everyday Meals Made Extraordinary / by Melina Davies— 1st ed.
 p. cm.
ISBN: 978-1-945551-71-0
1. Cooking 2. Cooking: Entertaining. I. Title.

Photography by Ann Elliott Cutting
Additional photography by Ashley Barrett
Photography of Davies children on dedication page by Bryan Randall
Line illustrations by Christian Davies

Designed by Amy Inouye, Future Studio

First edition, first printing

Printed in Korea